CAREFREE COOKING

CAREFREE COOKING

BY JACQUELYN REINACH

Hearthside Press Inc.

Publishers • New York

TO HARRY,

Who tried everything, including Eggs Mongole,
And paid for the house besides

CONTENTS

Acknowledgments

Carefree Cooking was conceived out of frustration when I was first faced with the problems of surviving, coping and cooking in our own vacation house. Thinking I was not alone in my struggle, I sent a questionnaire to people in second houses all over the country. Many of the solutions, styles and recipes have come from them . . . including the idea that a vacation house is more a state of mind than a particular place. So if you don't have a second house but want to cook the carefree way, throw a little sand in the food and you can swear you're living at the beach!

My special thanks to:

Sandra Erlbaum Abrams, New York City
Mr. & Mrs. Jaap Bar-David, Tel Aviv, Israel
Miss Helen Barrow, Southampton, New York
Mrs. William Chatfield, Rockport, Maine
Mrs. Ruth Ellen Church, Chicago, Illinois (Mary Meade, Chicago Tribune)
Mrs. Howard Cohen, Easthampton, New York
Mrs. Leo Cohen, Westhampton, New York
Mrs. Edith Hills Coogler, Food Editor of the Atlanta Journal
Mr. Jerry Cook, New York City
Mr. & Mrs. B. J. Corrigan, Bridgehampton, New York
The Disposables Association
Mrs. Helen Dreyfuss, New York City
Mrs. E. E. Dyett, Arlington, Vermont
Mr. and Mrs. Robert Goldscheider, Salisbury, Connecticut
Mrs. Sam Guttman, San Jose, California

Mr. Bill Harris, Paterson, New Jersey
Mr. & Mrs. Arnold Hoffman, Springs, New York
Mrs. Julian Hoffman, Bridgehampton, New York
Mr. & Mrs. Gordon Hyatt, New York City
Grace Teed Kent, New York City
Mrs. William Konecky, Shelter Island, New York
Mrs. Albert Krasne, Omaha, Nebraska
Mrs. Donald Krasne, Beverly Hills, California
Mrs. Lawrence Krasne, Council Bluffs, Iowa
Mrs. Marvin Lamport, Mount Kisco, New York
Miss Sibille Lerche, Heidelberg, Germany
Miss Dorothy Lerner, New York City
Miss Eleanor Lynch, Easthampton, New York
Dr. David Luck, Bridgehampton, New York
Mr. & Mrs. William Mayleas
Mr. & Mrs. Bert Margolis, Pittsfield, Mass.
Mr. Ed Mueller, Bridgehampton, New York
Mrs. James Otto, New York City
Pan-American Coffee Bureau
Mr. Ed Padula, Bridgehampton, New York
Mr. Gabriel Perle, New York City
Ronson Corporation
Mrs. Howard Rosenfeld, Tucson, Arizona
Mrs. Geraldine Salant, Paris, France
Mrs. May Webb Stephens, Lake Charles, Louisiana
(Food Editor, "Camping Guide" Magazine)
Mrs. Jeremy Tarcher (Shari Lewis) Beverly Hills, Calif.
The Tea Council of U.S.A., Inc.
Mr. & Mrs. Luiz Thedim, Rio de Janeiro, Brazil
Mrs. Charles T. Throop, Nashua, New Hampshire
Mrs. Charles Walcutt, Paris, France
Mrs. J. A. F. Wendt, Aspen, Colorado

And particularly:

Mr. and Mrs. Clyde Krasne, Beverly Hills, California, my parents, whose child psychology was "if you're a good girl, you can cook dinner!" (Funny, this doesn't work with my own children.)

Mrs. Nedda Casson Anders, a most patient and constructive editor-publisher, made the work of getting a manuscript into print seem carefree—even when it wasn't.

1

SURVIVAL,
Vacation-House Style

"Be Careful What You Wish For, You May Get It."
Old French Saying

"Come to the beautiful —————— (mountains, beach, hidden lake, deserted desert, choose one) and come prepared to stay. It's pure playground where you can own your own year-round vacation home . . . you can swim or ski or hunt or hike. Or relax . . . doing nothing is sometimes more fun than anything here . . ."

Advertisement, New York Times

"61% of all murders, suicides, and calls to the divorce lawyer—not to mention general family squabbles—occur during the accelerated emotional dynamics of leisure time."

A statistic I made up because it
feels that way sometimes

Emerson wasn't talking about Chinese cooking when he said "there's always some sour with the sweet."

Owning or renting a second house seems so luxurious, doesn't it, as you lie in your apartment bathtub, envisioning that get-away-from-it-all place where you can turn off the world, gaze at clouds, and have your family snug and secure.

Unfortunately, by the time you

pack
get the car loaded
drive to where you're going
stop on the way, or market after you get there (which I'll
    get to in a minute)
put away groceries
unpack
scrub bathrooms
make beds
arrange flowers
cook breakfast, followed by lunch, followed by dinner, followed by breakfast, and so forth

do dishes
wind the eight-day antique clock
sweep
clean
throw out flowers
take out garbage

When do you *relax?* When do you make love? When do you ever feel like it?
Something's got to give. You will have to develop . . .

A New Psychology

I don't know about you, but it took me years to stop feeling guilty if I didn't make the beds on Sundays. Not that I'm generally for not making beds, but who's going to tell?

Vacation Houses are places not to feel guilty in:

If you don't cook five-course Sunday dinners,
If you do use paper plates, paper cups, paper mats, paper anything (they're even making paper sheets and pillow-cases for guest rooms now),
If you let the dishes pile up while you enjoy the sunset,
If you want to spend all day Saturday cooking up a Drop Dead Dinner (see page 154),
If you don't want to spend all day Saturday cooking up a Drop Dead Dinner.

Vacation Houses are places not to be a martyr in:

Cook if you *want* to. Open cans if you *want* to. But staying home from clamming to bake a lemon meringue pie which nobody needs in the first place just so you can say "look what I did while you were all out having fun" is a bad game.

Vacation Houses are places to be happy *in:*

Put a radio in the kitchen. Pour a glass of wine. Enjoy yourself when you're cooking. That's where it's at.

Styles are Different the Second Time Around

Vacation-House happiness really starts in recognizing that you're dealing with new ways of life. Your marketing, eating times, meal-planning, company manners, cooking techniques—in short, your whole approach to housekeeping —are often quite different from those you're used to in your first house. Keeping the old habits for your first house and incorporating the new for your second (or for both) is the challenge. Think of yourself as a juggler. You've got one ball up in the air. Now's the time to start a second ball going and you handle it differently.

From the questionnaire that was sent out before this book was written, and from the many people whose brains I've picked, it seems there are options in all phases of second-house-running. Knowing the options helps you shift from one technique to another as necessity dictates; if you don't have time to market some weekend, perhaps you'll cook out of cans. And if you don't want to spend time marketing another weekend, perhaps you'll cook enough ahead so you won't worry about food. And if you do feel like marketing, you'll handle your meals differently. In a word, *flexibility.*

To Market, To Market—Vacation-House Style

A second house gives you a second place to shop, or really a third, because, clearly, you can market (a) in the "city" before you leave, (b) en route, spotting local fruit and vegetable stands, specialty stores, etc. (assuming they are still open after you've crept, tortoise-pace, out to beyond the parkway) and, finally, (c) from your local stores, if there are any, after you arrive.

Myself, I favor a judicious mixture of all three, more or less as follows:

In the city (or vicinity of House ⚹1):

When my time permits, I like to get a headstart on staples and canned goods loaded into the trunk of the car and out of the way. I actually market for both houses at once and ask the check-out clerk in the market to pack the foods in separate bags.

City marketing is the most important if your second house is quite far away from any shopping centers, because city prices will then probably be lower. Also the stock moves faster, and so the contents of boxes and cans will be fresher.

In the city is also the place to pick up a fabulous dessert and a great bread from your favorite bakery; and to stock up on gourmet specialty items you may be fond of.

En Route:

Couples and families who head for their second houses after working hours on Friday won't have the chance, but when we do, I patronize every reputable fruit and vegetable stand on our beat. The good ones really do sell fresh produce from nearby farms; others, of course, are rural outlets, twice removed from the A&P. These you skip. But from the real-McCoy places, buy fresh food, not only for your vacation house, but for bringing back to the city as well. Wonderful things like locally prepared chutney, honey of the region, and pickles and jams, as well as fruits and vegetables. On rainy Sundays we sometimes "mosey" back to the city early, stopping at the dairy farm for fresh eggs, milk and cream; the farm stand; the fish market (a shed in the back of Scotty's house where Montauk lobsters and local clams, mussels and scallops make choosing almost impossible); and some-times the doughnut shop.

After you've gotten there:

It's best to buy highly perishable foods such as fish, ham-burger, cream and milk as close to on-location as possible. But I travel with an insulated bag so that leftover perish-ables can survive the trip between houses 1 and 2 (why waste the quart of milk in your apartment over a week-end?) and vice-versa.

If you have a local supermarket, check the hours they are open and you may create another option for your marketing times. If you decide to let the marketing go till you get there, check your car space before you buy. We have often spent the last half hour's drive buried under grocery bags, forget-ting that a car full of passengers and luggage will only hold so many groceries. Incidentally, a time-saving operation for family marketing is to give everyone a different group of foods to buy—breadstuffs, meats, canned goods, and so forth. Meet at the check-out counter. (We've gotten this down to 22 minutes when we all pay attention!)

Next, a seemingly minor point, but one worth making: I cut down on bulk and simultaneously on work-time in the kitchen by buying second-house food stripped for action. The butcher trims surplus fat off the meat. At the farm stand, leaves and bottoms come off carrots, although I won't purchase them unless the foliage is on to begin with. But I *won't* let corn be husked unless we're having it the same day. Having childhooded in Iowa, I'm committed to the custom of blowing a whistle when the water's boiling. *Then* pick the corn and husk it!

And a public confession which more people ought to con-fess: If we get a late start and know we're going to arrive later and exhausted as well as hungry, or when I'm feeling lazy, I buy ready-fried or barbecued chickens in the city, or pick up a spit-roasted duckling along the way, or stop off for a bag of delicatessen meats. To those of you who have told me (and I can't quite reconstruct the tone of voice), "Oh, I *never* do *that*," I say, "so what!"

Finally. Unless you're spending a length of time in your vacation house, how do you remember, from one spell to another, what you've got and what you need? When you're planning menus in your first house, it's almost impossible to remember whether there's some saffron for the rice in your second. My own pseudo-scientific solutions are as follows:

One, make a marketing list while you are in your second house and put it in the glove compartment of your car. Or, two, keep a special purse and put the list in that, dropping in addenda as you think of things; then when it's time to market, all you have to remember is where you put the purse. Or, three, make a marketing list wherever you happen to be, and if in doubt, buy, on the theory that you can always use the food somewhere.

The marketing list on page 245 covers the basics for the good vacation-house life. Get your husband to Xerox a dozen or 30 copies; each time you market, use a copy to check off your needs.

About Serving and Eating Styles

Nobody says you have to have three meals a day. Or sit-down dinners. Why not eat when you feel like it, and in any style that's convenient? (See "Weekends At A Glance," page 103.)

Particularly when you entertain, consider the style. *How* you do it becomes as important as what you do:

Buffet Style

Put "buffet style" at the top of the list for vacation house entertaining. With so many serve-and-keep-warm appliances now available, you're free to party indoors or out with dozens of people. Call it a Smorgasbord, if you will. Or a Zakusky (which is really a Russian spread of hors-d'oeuvres after which you don't need to eat anything else, except the Russians always do). Or a Sideboard. Or a Groaning Board. It's one of the few styles that lets you be a guest at your own party.

Taverna Style

Another stylish but simple way of handling a large dinner party is to serve "taverna," from the kitchen, as the Greeks do. Plan your menu around casseroles or one-dish stews— perhaps three different kinds for a large group. Leave the pots right on the stove. When you're ready to eat, your guests go into the kitchen and help themselves directly from the pots.

Basket Style

With a collection of baskets, you can pack up all kinds of hand-held foods (hot chicken or spareribs will keep warm in Baggies or foil) and picnic on the porch or down by the lake. Or even right in the living room. Cover the tops of the baskets with napkins.

Whatever style you choose, enjoy. That's what it's all about, isn't it? One couple we know, for lack of a babysitter in a rather spread-out house, brought the baby right to the table and made him the centerpiece, cradle and all. Joey slept through the entire party.

About Cooking Styles

Here's where the juggling act really begins. *When* you do your second-house cooking is almost as important as *what* you do in terms of your freedom and fun.

The one thing you want to avoid is standing over a hot stove all day (unless it's pouring rain and you happen to like that sort of thing). So, when you're menu-planning and contemplating a recipe, ask yourself these questions (which I've tried to answer in my own recipes herewith):

1. Can I cook this recipe ahead of time?
2. Will it freeze?
3. Will cooking a double amount of this recipe give me a start on another dish? (Such as meat for sandwiches over the weekend. See "Leftovers You Plan.")
4. Can I cook this at the last minute?
5. Can I get some of the mess out of the way ahead of time and finish it off at dinner time?
6. Is it so good it's worth making however long it takes to cook?

Pay Now, Play Later: Cooking Ahead

This is a style I try to live by whenever it's practical, which means having the time. Cook ahead the dishes or cooked foods you need for a recipe (such as cold boiled lobster for a future salad). Almost anything you can think of—meats, desserts, sauces, salad dressings—can be made two or three days ahead of time (longer with a freezer).

Mae Webb Stephens, Food Editor of "Camping Guide" Magazine, has worked out some useful ideas for her trailer weekends. (Some trailer with an oven, ice-box, freezer and airconditioning!) She says: "I prepare salad greens, vegetables and fruits before I leave home. Wash and drip-dry lettuce; wash celery; scrub carrots, etc., and put them all in an airtight container in the ice-box . . . I let meats that I plan to barbecue marinate on the way . . . buy frozen pies ready to make, and take them in their cartons. Making a crust is messy and takes a lot of time."

1. COOK AHEAD IN YOUR FIRST HOUSE and carry food to your second. (See "Have Food, Will Travel" following.)

2. COOK AHEAD IN YOUR SECOND HOUSE: Rainy mornings are fine times to get caught up. Whether you have a freezer or not doesn't really matter. There are so many stews, ragouts,

en daubes, goulashes, stroganoffs, currys, whatever, that improve with two or three days' ripening time, don't worry.

3. REVERSAL: COOK AHEAD IN YOUR VACATION HOUSE TO CARRY FOOD BACK TO THE CITY. This works for working wives who have more time to cook on weekends. It works for when you've got painters in your apartment, or a hectic week coming up.

4. COOK DOUBLE: If you have a freezer in either house, you can save time, not only by cooking ahead, but by cooking double amounts when you do. Have the first meal right away. Freeze the second meal for another time.

We've even gotten into the habit of barbecuing an extra steak when we cook out. We tuck it into our small above-the-refrigerator freezer and have it ready to pull out for a Sunday night, or travelling-day cookless meal.

You can also cook double and save time when you make: spaghetti sauces; soups; curries; stews; cakes; pies; and any cooked meat.

Have Food, Will Travel

Once you've cooked ahead, the easiest way to transport a main dish is in a covered casserole. Tape around the edges if there's a lot of liquid.

You'll find an insulated bag (they come in both soft-collapsible and hard versions these days) a wonderful help for collecting and protecting the food you carry. The important rule is, *never travel more than two hours* with unrefrigerated *cooked* foods. The insulated bag will get you out of the danger zone.

More Travel Hints

1. If you want to carry cooked foods and not bother lugging casserole dishes, use *disposable plastic bags* or *foil*. Double-wrap, if there's a lot of liquid.

2. *Frozen foods can defrost on the way.*
3. *Foods that need marinating* can soak up flavor in plastic bags as you're travelling.
4. *Use Baggies* to carry bits of things you might be taking: condiments, small amounts of herbs you don't want to bother duplicating, nuts.
5. *Salads,* without dressing, can travel in plastic bags. Carry the dressing separately in a covered container.
6. *If you want to keep foods cold* without an insulated container, freeze water in plastic containers with lids, and put one in a box or basket with your food.

Second-House Housekeeping or How to be Carefree While Cleaning

Somebody once said, "A house is a machine for living in," but sometimes you wonder who's the machine, you or the house? It's even more wonderable in the second house where you arrive fresh, or, rather, stale, from having coped with all your first house problems.

But unless you're prepared to rough it, obviously somebody's got to make the second-house-machine work. And that somebody is you. While this is a cookbook and not a housekeeping book, it's clear that your food problems are a part of general housekeeping problems. So here is a sampling of the decisions and options that will help make life lovelier the second house around.

Rules, expectations, and a job for everyone help make life much easier. Decide:

Who does what chores? (For example, everybody makes his own bed in our house; I cook; my husband helps me clean up; the kids take turns cleaning their bathroom.)

When does the work get done? (Right after breakfast is a good time, for example.)

What's really important? What can be skipped?

What kind of timesavers can be invented? (Such as lining

each wastebasket with a plastic bag for quick disposal; keeping a sponge and small can of cleansing powder in the bathroom to avoid extra steps; using paper towels in the bathroom to cut down on laundry; keeping loose ice cubes in a plastic bag in the icecube section of your refrigerator (see page 68.)

General Cleaning

This should be planned to suit your life. If you're summering, for instance, and expect a lot of weekend guests, try to get the cleaning out of the way before you get involved with weekend marketing and cooking. I prefer thorough cleaning on Mondays (after everybody's gone) and a quick swipe on Thursdays. You might want to reverse matters.

Laundry

Again, this has to be a decision. Do you have the facilities in your home? Do you collect a pile for the laundromat? Some weekenders we know find it easier to cart everything to the city and back again.

Being Prepared

Keep a list of the local people who will service your various appliances and make house repairs as needed. Fill in the telephone list on page 30 and keep a duplicate list in your first house.

One of our neighbors has typed out and posted general house rules which serve as reminders to the family and hints to younger-set guests. You could needlepoint them, too!

REMINDERS:

1. Do not put into toilets anything but toilet tissue.
2. *Especially* do not put cigarette butts into toilets or sinks.
3. Do not use too much suds in washing machine.
4. Do not pour oil or other fats into sink.

5. Do not put tea leaves or coffee grounds into sink. (The above is due to the fact that these things will muck up our small septic tank.)
6. Do not wash sandy items in sinks or appliances. Use the outdoor hose to rinse them out.
7. Last one to sleep: Please check stove to make sure it is off. Please turn out lights.

Weekend Opening and Closing

Weekending, or part-time use of your house, poses new options. Once you make them and get into a regular routine, you'll feel much more carefree about the whole business and a little smug (at least I do, having spent the first few months waking up in terror in my first house, thinking I'd left the stove on in the second).

Cleaning Schedules

Do you arrive and start cleaning? Do you clean up before you leave? Can you manage to find a local high-school girl who might come in during the week and tidy up for a couple of hours?

These are the options. We prefer to bustle around the last hour on a Sunday and leave a clean house to come back to—it's also safer. One of the nice things about weekend housekeeping is that the weekly chores of a city apartment become monthly tasks. After all, you're not using the house that much, so that bed-changing, refrigerator cleaning, etc. do not have to be done every week.

Laundry

Leave dirty clothes and bedding (if you leave them) spread out somewhere to get air, and you won't have a mildew problem. If clothes do get musty, a good laundering or cleaning should remedy.

Dampness in General

If your vacation house is prone to dampness, there are many commercial sprays for clothing and furniture that will help keep moisture out and mold down. You can also buy small bags of a calcium product to keep in bureau drawers. Some of my friends have even used chalk successfully to combat that "heavy feeling" on the linen shelves. It also helps to leave closet doors and bureau drawers open when you leave.

What to Do About Electricity and Heat

Whether you leave electricity and heat on during the week is really more a matter of emotional safety rather than physical safety. There is no reason you have to be concerned if you simply close the front door (having checked to make certain the stove is off) and leave everything on. We prefer, because we have circuit breakers, to flip off everything except the refrigerator. (We marked our refrigerator circuit with tape after once turning it off by mistake and returning to find a gloppy spoiled mess!) Other friends prefer to turn off the stove and hot water heater only. This is a case where you find out what's comfortable for *you* to live with.

If your house is in a climate where the pipes might freeze, then you will have to make provisions. If your heating system permits, leave the thermometer set at 55°. Otherwise you will have to have the water turned off during the cold season.

WINTER PIONEERING: Our friends, the Goldscheiders, have worked out this system for the three months they must turn off the water in their Connecticut country house. Their propane-fueled heating system is not large enough to heat the house week-round. So they carry in 10 gallons of water per weekend. This is enough to pour into the toilets (which will then flush) and to heat for other needs. Before leaving on a weekend, they pour a little kerosene into the toilets which further insures that the waste matter will disappear.

Beginning of the Weekend Checklist

1. Is there food for the first meal?
2. Is there food to be moved from freezer to refrigerator?
3. Do icecubes need changing? Refrigerator need airing?
4. Is there toilet paper? Soap?
5. (If this affects you:) Is fuel supply operable? Are all the circuits on? Is hot water tank on?

End of the Weekend Checklist

1. Are perishable foods disposed of? (Freeze bacon, butter, bread, milk, etc. Throw out dribs and drabs. Pack up worthwhile leftovers to take back. See "Leftovers", in index.)
2. Are the plants watered?
3. Are all windows and doors locked?
4. Is garbage disposed of? Wastebaskets emptied?
5. Is the stove turned off? Lights? (Unless you feel strongly about leaving one or two lights on an automatic timer to discourage prowlers.)
6. Is laundry arranged for?

Seasonal Opening and Closing

The crazy-making aspect of getting your vacation house opened or closed is that while opening one, you may be closing the other. And vice-versa. Or you may not be closing your first house, but may be leaving a husband who commutes on weekends.

At any rate, the easiest way of handling the situation, I think, is to deal with both houses at once, item by item as the situation calls for it.

Arranging for Services

Depending on your needs, decide what you're going to do about the following for one or both houses:

Mail—how to be handled

Newspaper—delivery arrangements

Milk Delivery—stopped or started

Telephone—You may want to have your first house telephone temporarily disconnected if you'll be gone any length of time. Arrange for service in your vacation house. When stopping service, have it stopped the day *after* you leave. A telephone is handy to have up till the last minute.

Other regular delivery services—such as laundry, cleaners, garbage collection.

Plumbing System

On leaving: turn off the water supply over a winter. Drain toilets, sinks, bathtubs, pipes (outdoor ones, too) and hot water heater to prevent damage from freezing. Before reconnecting, check to see if hot water heater needs cleaning out.

Electricity and Gas

Arrange to have these services started or stopped. Check your fuel supply if you use another system. Disconnect bottled fuel supply on leaving.

House Repairs

Have chimneys and flues checked before opening your house. Repair screens, if necessary; put up or take down screens. Arrange for repairs that might be needed.

Clean and Safe Closing

It's a temptation, at the end of a season, to walk out the door and plan to clean up your house when you open up again. However, a thorough cleaning—vacuuming of furniture and mattresses—storing of rugs, etc.—is valuable insurance against weather, insects, dampness and dust.

SAFETY PRECAUTIONS: Throw out oily rags, stacks of newspapers, whatever might be considered a fire hazard. Lock all windows and doors securely. Leave a key with a neighbor in case of emergencies.

WHAT TO DO ABOUT FOOD: Dispose of bits and open boxes of food. I'm inclined to dispose of everything—either throwing out or taking back to the city. Let's face it, all those little bottles of herbs are going to get stale over a winter anyway. However, if you want to store a few staples or canned goods, put staples in a metal container with a tight-fitting cover. Wrap canned goods in an old rug or blankets, or several layers of newspapers. This is because paper boxes may attract mice and insects; cans may burst in extreme cold.

WHAT TO DO ABOUT BEDDING, LINEN, CLOTHING: Leave everything clean and in as dry a place as possible. I haven't found it necessary to bother with packing anything away. I simply strew bags of a commercial calcium product in and around the closets and linen shelves.

About Linens and Bedding for Your Vacation House

Two sets of *sheets* and pillowcases for each bed are enough if you do your laundry locally. You'll do better with three, if you carry laundry back to the city. The no-iron sheets and pillowcases are heaven-sent.

Blankets will depend on the climate, obviously. Keep 1 to 2 extra for each bed if you have cold nights. Being cold is awful!

Sleeping bags are a good solution for many house-guests, particularly the under-twenty ones.

Towels: We've found it easier to eliminate all the small towels such as hand towels or anything fancy. Use paper towelling. Stick to one-size bath towels, and washcloths for those who use them. Oversized beach towels, of course, are needed for beach and lake homes, and you always need more than you think.

I find I need about 8–10 *dish towels,* and have eliminated dishcloths by using the throwaway kind or sponges.

Emergencies

First Aid

The best first aid in your second house is to be prepared. The following list indicates the basic first aid supplies you should stock. The telephone list on page 30 provides space for doctor's and emergency hospital's numbers. You might do well, also, to keep a first aid book handy to cover the numerous small, but annoying, situations that may arise with your being far away from a doctor.

FIRST AID AND EMERGENCIES

... Alka Seltzer
... Antiseptic
... Aspirin
... Band-aids
... Candles
... Fire Extinguisher (see page 29)
... First Aid Book
... Flashlight
... Gauze pads

... Lotion for insect bites
... Mouth-to-mouth resuscitator (particularly for boat owners)
... Ointment for burns
... Thermometer
... Tool Chest: Hammer, screwdriver, nails, picture hooks, Scotch tape, freezer tape, soft pencil for writing on tape

If Your Power Fails

Keep fuses on hand, in case the failure is within the house. Where a storm might cut power in the entire area, the best you can do is keep some kind of portable heating equipment for cooking, and a good supply of wood for fireplace heat.

COOKING IN A STORM:

1. The new "portable chefs" which operate on butane gas will provide controlled heat if your electric stove is not operating.
2. Sterno will heat a small amount of food.

3. Chafing dishes and fondue dishes that work on alcohol stay usable.
4. Your outdoor equipment—hibachi, brazier, or barbecue grill can pinch-hit once the storm is over. A small hibachi that fits into the fireplace is good anytime. (See index for "Winter Cook-In.")

WHAT TO DO WITH FROZEN FOODS?

1. Keep your freezer door closed. Your freezer will keep food frozen for 48 hours if warm air is not admitted.
2. If your power failure goes on beyond 48 hours, add dry ice to your freezer. Leave the dry ice in large pieces. Place on top of each shelf of food, so the cold air will flow downwards.
3. If you cannot get dry ice, consider moving a large freezer-full to a frozen food locker.
4. Check the frozen foods: If foods have thawed only partially and there are still ice crystals in the package, they may be safely refrozen. But use as soon as possible.

Fire

Include an operating fire extinguisher in your basic kitchen supplies. It should be a dry chemical or a CO_2 extinguisher to work for any kind of fire.

COMMON KITCHEN FIRES: If grease in a skillet catches fire, turn off the heat. If possible, put a lid on the skillet. If need be, smother the fire with baking soda or salt.

If you have an oven fire, turn off the heat and close the door. This cuts off the air supply and smothers the fire.

Purifying Water

If your water supply comes from a well or a spring, have it analyzed before you use it for drinking and cooking. If there is any doubt, purify water as follows:

Boil all drinking water for 10 minutes, or mix 2 table-

spoons household chlorine bleach to 5 gallons of water.
Store the water in glass, stone, or porcelain containers. Clean
the containers after each use.

Second House Telephone Directory

Emergency Numbers

Fire ————————————————————————————

Police ——————————————————————————

Doctor ——————————————————————————

Emergency Hospital————————————————————

Caretaker (someone who has the key) ————————————

Household Service

Plumber ——————————————————————————

Electrician ————————————————————————

Appliance Repairs ——————————————————————

Local Stores and Other Household Numbers

————————————————————————————————

————————————————————————————————

Local Friends

————————————————————————————————

————————————————————————————————

2

KITCHEN POWER:
Equipment and Supplies, and How to Improvise if Necessary

"Old Mother Hubbard went to the cupboard
To get her poor doggie a bone.
But when she got there,
The cupboard was bare . . ."
Pity she hadn't read this chapter.

With a well-stocked second kitchen, you and Mother Hubbard may part ways.

This is the kind of chapter most books relegate to fine print at front or back, and I grant you that reading lists is like reading the telephone book. But I urge you to consider that a carefully planned and stocked second kitchen is the first step towards getting out of the kitchen door.

The lists and ideas which follow are based on the assumption that there isn't going to be much space for mistakes— like those darling asparagus plates on sale which have sat on the top shelf in your first kitchen for two years. That you want the maximum mileage out of the minimum equipment. (Unless, as with some women, your second kitchen is larger and the place where you spend most of your cooking time, and collect all kinds of gourmet accoutrements, in which case you don't need this chapter.)

Basic Kitchen Equipment

In your second kitchen you need more of less, or less of more, as Chinese philosophers might say.

1. Casseroles

Pick your casseroles to go from refrigerator or freezer to stove to table and back and maybe travel in the car with you. It's silly to have to keep transferring food from one container to another. Check to see that the casseroles you do buy have tight-fitting covers and can be used on top of the stove as well as in the oven. Some can't.

The porcelain enamel-on-steel casseroles are beautifully made, come in all kinds of colors, and suit the purpose just fine. You might consider 2–3 different sizes, depending on the size of your family. (Our family of four does nicely with 2 basic covered casseroles—a 1-quart and a 4-quart.)

2. Pots and Pans

Choose for flexibility. Buy frying pans and saucepans with covers for greater use. Avoid like the plague the copper-bottom stuff that's impossible to keep clean, particularly in salt air. Teflon or not is up to you. I like the heavy aluminum pots and pans (even though you have to be careful of the handles) because they can slide into the oven if need be, and don't get hurt sitting over a barbecue.

3. Oversized Pots

Depending again on the life you lead, think about owning one or two oversized pots (such as a large soup kettle which can also cook corn for a crowd; or a clam steamer) for entertaining crowds. See page 37 for hints on improvising equipment for a crowd.

4. Disposable Equipment

Bear in mind that you can buy almost any kind of disposable specialized cooking equipment these days—aluminum foil bread pans, cookie sheets, muffin tins, cake pans, roasting pans, etc. And think of the washing up you won't have to do.

5. Electric and Self-Fueling Equipment

There are some marvelous kinds of cooking and serving equipment available now that free you up to cook at the table, outdoors, anywhere. Whether electric or propane-fueled, consider it well worth the investment to have at least one cooking and one serving piece, such as an electric frying pan AND an electric warming tray. At the least, invest in some inexpensive candle warmers to use for buffet and outdoor meals.

The one other electric thing I'd opt for is a blender, which does me more good at the beach than in the city.

6. Your Kitchenware

Of course your own preferences are going to hold sway here. This is my minimum list. Beware of kitchen gadgets; you simply don't need them (and you can always improvise).

Mixing bowls: If they're made of metal or of ceramic they can double as double boilers

Chopping board or bowl

Coffee pot: Electric percolators can keep coffee warm over a morning

Egg beater, and I like a wire whisk in addition

Garlic press

All-purpose grater-slicer

Knife sharpener

Knives: At least 3 in varying sizes

Measuring cups: Pyrex two-cup and four-cup

Measuring spoons

Openers: A bottle opener and a can opener

Pot holders

Salt and pepper shakers

Sifter and/or strainer and/or colander: one or all of these depending on whether or not you sift and strain. I find one large wire colander works for me for draining foods, sifting flour, etc.

Scissors: for mincing almost any herb; cutting chickens; cutting flowers, etc.

Spatula

Spoons: I prefer 2 to 3 wooden spoons for mixing

Tea kettle (optional): You can always boil water in a saucepan

Large tongs: Good for lifting corn on the cob out of boiling water; steaks off of hot barbecue grills, etc.

Vegetable peeler

7. Your Tableware

Who here among us is lucky enough to start from scratch? Most of us end up with the remnants of three different sets of crockery and a shelf full of jelly glasses.

However, if you're shopping for new, consider investing in metal plates (expensive, but marvelous as they can sit in the oven, retain heat, and never break!). And unbreakable glasses which now come in rather chic patterns. (I do not like plastic dinnerware, because I swear I can taste the plastic after awhile, but perhaps it's rude of me to say so.)

Placemats—of washable plastic or heavy woven stuff (which keeps cleaner longer than you might think).

Napkins—Why bother with anything except paper?

Cutlery—Stainless steel can be had in any price range, and you won't feel so bad if a spoon gets lost outdoors.

8. Serving Aids

Trays—for the perpetual carting, and to double as serving dishes for parties. Cover them with foil.

A large salad bowl, which all-purposes for breads, desserts, clams, etc., as well as salad.

Wicker baskets—they always seem to come in handy for anything from breads to picking flowers.

Wooden board—excellent for cheeses; slicing bread.

One wooden meat platter which catches the juices.

9. For the Oven

Given enough casseroles, the only pan you absolutely need is an oven broiler pan with a slotted rack. And a roaster, if you can bring yourself to buy the foil ones when needed.

10. For the Barbecue

Long-handled fork
Barbecue mitt
   All the sophisticated equip-ment—wire grills, basters, aprons and hats and so forth —are entirely up to you.

11. For the Bar

Icebucket
Church key opener
Wine bottle opener
Shaker or blender
Glasses

12. For Storage

Depending on the climate where your second house is located, you may want to invest in glass canisters or apothecary jars with ground glass tops. They will protect many foods from dampness. (A good way to remember basic directions for foods you transfer, such as pancake mix or rice, is to tear off the back of the original carton. Tuck it into the jar along with the food, or tape it to the outside.)

You should also have a supply of plastic bags and containers which are invaluable for travelling as well as storage.

How to Avoid Mother Hubbard's Bare Cupboard

Devising a plan of marketing and menus for your house may seem like a chore, but careful planning makes the carefree life possible. Without it, you may begin to feel you're paying rent to the A&P.

The system that has worked for us has been one of starting with a well-stocked house from opening day on, and then planning as needed. (See "To Market, To Market")

If you're a weekender only, the approach can be the same.

Just once, before you open the house, sit down, list the basic staples you need, go to the supermarket *alone* (you'll never remember everything with the kids throwing Bosco into the cart) and stock up. Carefree-ness is getting the basics into the house so your mind is free to think only in terms of particular meals as you go along.

Plan a Survival Shelf

In addition to stocking up on staples, plan a shelf or part of a shelf for emergencies, which I call second-house survival. (See all the specifics in Chapter 5) On this shelf will go the canned or packaged makings for quick appetizers (page 81) or quick meals should you arrive late or tired or have drop-ins who stay for dinner. (See recipes starting on page 92.)

Opening the House Checklist

The checklist on page 245 outfits your house for the season. It looks like a lot, but it really isn't, and it's almost worth building a closet somewhere, or putting up pegboard (so you can get hangables out of precious shelf space which can then hold food) to give you enough room.

I use the list as my basic security, and have pretty much been able to group my thinking into two categories: a). do I need anything from the basic list? and b). what do I need for a particular menu? Obviously, I would be putting you on if I said this worked every week of the season, but it's a more than satisfactory beginning to take off from.

You may object to my spice list. So let me make mention of the fact that herbs spoil so quickly (*when* will they start packaging them in really tiny bottles?) I'd rather buy the more exotic ones for a recipe as I go along. Also, in the summer, try keeping them in the refrigerator. They'll stay fresher.

Also, I do very little baking in our beach house, preferring to save my time for sauces. You may want to extend your baking supplies.

How to Make a Whiskey Bottle into a Rolling Pin and Other Ways of Improvising Equipment to Cook and Serve With

Improvising Cooking Equipment

Unless your second-house kitchen is where you do most of your cooking (some women like to cook on weekends, for example, and take food back for the week), chances are you're going to not have something you want for a recipe. (Also see "Have Food, Will Travel")

When this happens, first thing is to cast a very appraising eye at flowerpots, garden equipment, empty bottles and so forth and see what you can invent. (Don't forget the kitchen-saving uses of aluminum foil. A piece wrapped triple thickness around a shirt cardboard can be a quick cookie sheet if you're caught with your cookie sheets down.) Just for example:

Make a rolling pin by wrapping foil around a whiskey bottle. If the bottle is empty, fill it with water.

Make a meat tenderizer from a hammer or a brick.

Make pot lids for anything from foil.

Use safety pins to "sew-up" chicken or turkey.

Make a potato masher from a soda bottle. Just mash with the bottle.

Cooking for a crowd. If you don't have enough pans, use large plastic garbage bags to marinate meat, hold vegetables. Use a large roasting pan to hold a frozen or chilled dessert. When ready to serve, wrap foil around the pan. Serve as is.

Bake cakes in empty 2-pound coffee cans. Line them with foil, first, so the batter won't stick.

Save jars and bottles for containers (refrigerator and pantry shelf)

Improvising Serving Dishes

A hollowed-out cabbage can hold an appetizer dip, a cocktail sauce for shrimp, a can of sterno to make a living room hibachi for appetizers. Put the food you're dipping or broiling on toothpicks. Stick the picks around the outside of the cabbage.

A wheelbarrow lined with foil can hold iced drinks—sodas and beer for a party. Heap barrow with ice. Lay the bottles on top.

Scooped-out orange shells can be serving bowls for ice cream; or to mold jello in. You can also fill them with chicken salad, and so forth for individual buffet service.

Make "trees" to hold food such as shrimp or vegetables for a buffet table. Stud a pineapple with toothpicks holding chunks of whatever food you're using.

Collect large beach shells and use them as dishes for salads, desserts, individual ramekins.

Small clay flower pots can make charming dishes for serving ice creams and sherbets. Fill the pots just before serving, or fill them ahead of time and freeze. Serve on individual paper plates or saucers. Stick flowers into every pot and call it a garden coming to the table.

Emergency Food Substitutions*

If you don't have this	Use this
Baking powder, 1 teaspoon sulfate-phosphate	1½ teaspoons phosphate baking powder; or 2 teaspoons tartrate baking powder
Butter, 1 cup for shortening	⅞ cup lard, or rendered fat with ½ teaspoon salt; or 1 cup hydrogenated fat with ½ teaspoon salt
Chocolate, 1 square (ounce)	3 tablespoons cocoa plus 1 tablespoon fat
Corn syrup, 1 cup	1 cup sugar plus ¼ cup liquid
Cream (for cooking)	
1 cup heavy cream	⅓ cup butter plus ¾ cup milk
1 cup light cream	3 tablespoons butter plus ¾ cup milk
Eggs, 1 whole egg for thickening or baking	2 egg yolks. Or 2½ tablespoons sifted dried whole egg plus 2½ tablespoons water
Flour:	
For thickening: 1 tablespoon	½ tablespoon cornstarch, potato starch. Or 2 teaspoons quick-cooking tapioca
For baking, 1 cup cake flour	⅞ cup all-purpose flour
For breads, 1 cup all-purpose	Up to ½ cup bran, whole-wheat flour, or cornmeal plus enough all-purpose flour to fill cup
Garlic, I small clove	⅛ teaspoon garlic powder
Herbs, fresh, 1 tablespoon	½ to 1½ teaspoons dried (use less for the stronger flavored ones)
Honey, 1 cup	1 cup sugar plus ¼ cup liquid

If you don't have this	Use this
Milk: 1 cup buttermilk or sour milk for baking	1 cup sweet milk mixed with one of the following: 1 tablespoon vinegar. Or 1 tablespoon lemon juice. Or 1¾ teaspoons cream of tartar.
1 cup fluid whole milk	½ cup evaporated milk plus ½ cup water. Or 1 cup reconstituted dry whole milk. Or 1 cup reconstituted non-fat dry milk plus 2½ teaspoons butter
Mushrooms, 1 lb. fresh	3 oz. dried
Sugar, 1 cup	1 cup maple syrup or honey (reducing liquid in recipe by ¼ cup) 1 cup molasses (add ¼ teaspoon baking soda)
Yogurt, 1 cup	1 cup buttermilk

* Compiled from information from U. S. Department of Agriculture

If You're Cooking at High Altitudes

The higher your mountain chalet, the longer the cooking time to allow. (Something to do with the relationship of air pressure to the temperature at which water boils. The higher you go, the lower the air pressure, the sooner water boils, but the lower the temperature it boils at—so things never get as hot as they do at good old sea level and thus take longer to cook. And now you know why I almost flunked chemistry. If high altitudes are a year round problem for you, please consult some of the excellent books on the subject now available.)

In General

1. Allow more cooking time.

2. Add more liquid to soups, sauces, stews, etc. to allow for the added evaporation which takes place over a longer cooking time.
3. Use a pressure cooker (which is controllable) for as many foods as possible.
4. When baking, experiment with your oven at your particular altitude. Increase oven temperature to get the heat you need. And since the underweight air plays tricks on the delicate balance of cakes, add *more* flour and *less* baking powder the higher you go. (This is to keep your cake from flying out the window altogether.)

What to Do with Leftover Milk and All Kinds of Storage for All Kinds of Foods

Part of being carefree in your vacation house is *not* to find a penicillin-rich refrigerator or potatoes sprouting gaily in the sun. Because you may be coming and going, leaving foods behind you, the storage problem is important.

The list on page 233 will give you the most important storing and freezing information, and the handling of leftovers for basic foods.

Before getting down to specifics, consider this general approach: sometimes you find yourself with an icebox full of dribs and drabs, particularly at the end of a weekend. Or you bought extra milk because the Knudsens were dropping by with their kids, and then all the kids wanted were cokes. What do you do? What are your options?

Freezing and Storing

More foods than you'd think can keep quite nicely for long periods of time in the freezer or refrigerator. (Check the storage chart on page 233). Believe it or not, milk can be frozen. Freeze leftover vegetables in foil packets, ready to reheat for a quick children's dinner.

Taking Home

If you're weekending, the extra salad greens or uncooked corn, or whatever, can go into plastic bags and be taken home for Monday's dinner.

Inventing

Some foods just sit there in your refrigerator begging to be the stuff menu-dreams are made of. Last night's mashed potatoes can make lovely potato pancakes for breakfast. Cooked vegetables can go into salads, as well as into the freezer. Meat never seems to be a problem. Half the fun of cooking is to open the icebox, stare inside, and figure out new combinations. Why *can't* you mix three kinds of cooked vegetables in a curry sauce and be one up on tonight's dinner? (See Index for "In-a-Hurry Curry Sauce.")

Throwing Out

Some leftovers simply don't deserve more than a quick trip to the garbage can. Do what your conscience dictates, but be honest; are you really going to use that quarter cup of gravy (which can be frozen, incidentally, to lend flavor to a future soup or salad), or that tablespoon of cooked carrots? Here it's every man for himself, but the section on page 233 does have some suggestions for the leftover foods most likely to be found in your or my kitchen.

File this basic rule: *When In Doubt, Throw It Out!*

3

IF IT'S MORNING, IT MUST BE BREAKFAST . . .

or it might be Brunch or Lunch

"Oh, it's nice to get up in the mornin'
But it's nicer to lie in bed."

Sir Harry Lauder

Second House Breakfasts can be anytime from when the sun comes over the mountain to high noon. Or later; I think it depends on your metabolism.

But *your* metabolism may not be *their* metabolism. And *they* may want to get out to the ski slopes while you'd like to rest up from the week. Or vice-versa. Or you'd prefer black coffee and NO conversation while *they're* starved from the invigorating air of the (beach, mountains, lake, desert . . . pick one).

The obvious problem in breakfasting is flexibility. Whether you have houseguests or not (see Index "Weekend At a Glance"), morning is a matter of personal rhythms which have to be dealt with.

Coping With Breakfast Time, Assuming You're Not Alone

If You Like To Get Up Early

. . . there's really no problem. You have plenty of time to make coffee and prepare breakfast, or brunch, nibbling a bit to tide you over.

If Everybody Gets Up at the Same Time

. . . or you're lucky enough to have a set breakfast hour, you can rustle up an ordinary breakfast in 20 minutes. While everybody else is getting dressed, just don't, and you'll come out on time.

If You Like To Sleep Late

. . . this is the kicker. You're certainly entitled to your habits, but you have to plan a little for the habits of others which may include children, houseguests, or just your beloved. There are several options:

1. EVERYBODY WAITS. Theoretically it's possible. But not practical.

2. EVERYBODY GETS HIS OWN BREAKFAST . . . the first one up makes coffee. If you're lucky enough to have a guest with a culinary talent (as we were with the concoctor of the Potato Fritters which follow), prevail upon him or her to make his specialty.

You can help matters along by preparing some things the night before. Pancake batter or the makings of French toast can be ready in the refrigerator. Leave a pan on the stove with a spatula and a bottle of cooking oil nearby. People make their own as they feel like it.

3. EVERYBODY HELPS HIMSELF TO SOMETHING YOU'VE PRE-PARED TO TIDE HIM OVER, AND WAITS FOR YOU TO COOK BREAK-FAST, BRUNCH, OR LUNCH, DEPENDING ON WHAT TIME IT IS. This solution can work very well with husbands, houseguests, and children. You have to do some setting up exercises the night before, such as putting out: An electric coffeepot (the first one up plugs it in). Boxes of individual cereals (on a tray, with bowls, sugar, and perhaps some bananas). And/ or sweet rolls or coffee cake, covered with foil. A bowl of fruit.

Breakfast With Style

Even if you're like some people I know who can go 365 mornings on soft-boiled eggs and bacon, you can still carry a tray outdoors and enjoy the view.

With any kind of portable hot plate, or a keep-warm tray, your entire breakfast can be outdoors. Why not?

If There's a Crowd In the House

If you're loaded with houseguests, or simply have a large family, just making a simple bacon-and-egg breakfast can drive you to the nearest real estate agent. Pots . . . pans . . . waiting for toast to pop up . . . all of a sudden it's time to start dinner and you're not finished with breakfast!

Most of the menus which follow have been worked out to accommodate a lot of people. In addition, you may want to adapt some of these to two, when you're alone at last.

1. EGGS FOR A CROWD: Our best solution has been to bake eggs, which you can do 16–20 at a time in a large baking pan. Better still, use an aluminum foil pan. You can bake eggs in any kind of sauce from plain melted butter to a Stroganoff sauce (page 48) to a doctored canned soup. Try Shirred Eggs Mongole (page 50).

You can *scramble* lots of eggs in a double boiler, and you can make a double boiler out of a metal or ceramic mixing bowl set in a pan of water.

Beat your eggs (16 make about 4 cups) in the bowl you're going to use. Add butter and seasoning. Set the bowl into hot water. Stir frequently with a wooden spoon; 12 or more eggs will take 20–30 minutes to scramble.

2. BACON FOR A CROWD: Bake your bacon in one or two aluminum-foil broiling pans. If the bacon is very cold, put a slab into the pan. Start cooking. In about 5 minutes the bacon will be soft enough to separate with a fork. Total time will be about 20 minutes in a 350° oven.

3. NO-TOASTER TOAST FOR A CROWD (or if you don't have a toaster): Lay as many slices of bread as you need on a large foil pan or baking pan (with sides), or your oven broiler pan. Put a large hunk of butter (about 2 teaspoons) on each slice of bread. Bake the bread in a 400° oven for 15 to 20 minutes. The butter will permeate the bread, giving you a buttered slice of toast-on-the-bottom, soft-on-top. It's delicious!

If you've got more bread than pan, just put in the entire sliced loaf, and butter the top. Also delicious.

If you have unsliced bread, slice the loaf lengthwise. Spread with butter (and herbs, if desired). Bake 20 minutes.

4. COOKING AHEAD AND KEEPING WARM: Some foods, such as

pancakes, waffles, sausages, and French toast can be made ahead of time and kept warm in a very low oven.

ANYTIME BREAKFASTS

. . . bearing in mind that one man's breakfast is another man's Sunday supper.

> *Skewered Fruits**
> *Scrambled Eggs Plus**
> *Hot Rolls*
> *Coffee*

Here are some ways to glamorize plain old scrambled eggs. You can turn this menu into a brunch buffet by making two or more of the accompaniments and letting people choose their own to go with the eggs.

Skewered Fruits

String any combination of fruits you like on small skewers. Serve cold. Or make Grilled Fruit Kebobs (see Index). Use bananas, in chunks; pineapple chunks, fresh or canned; orange segments; prunes; figs; large berries.

Scrambled Eggs Plus

Scrambled eggs are good with almost anything you can think of in them or on them. The following are some ideas.

Beat as many eggs as you like (allowing 2 per person) with a whisk or fork. Add 1 teaspoon of cream or sour cream per egg, if you like (although we're of the "don't add anything school") for an eggier taste. Add a dash of salt and pepper. Scramble in butter in a pan or the top of a double boiler. Stir with a wooden spoon until set. Serve immediately.

PLUSES

1. *Chicken livers,* floured lightly and sautéed in butter. Add a dash of onion salt, a dash of vermouth. Serve on the side.

2. *Sautéed Onions:* Sauté onion rings in butter until soft. Mix them through the eggs just before the eggs are set.

3. *Sautéed Seafood:* Sauté shrimp, crabmeat, scallops or lobster meat in butter. Add a dash of onion salt and vermouth. Add to the eggs just before set.

4. *Sautéed sausages,* including chorizo, salami, or Italian sweet sausage. Dice the sausages and brown. Serve either on the side or in the eggs.

5. *Home fries:* Brown sliced potatoes and onions in butter until crisp. Serve on the side. (You can use leftover baked potatoes, too.)

6. *Sautéed mushrooms:* Sauté sliced mushrooms and onions in butter. Serve on top of a portion of eggs.

7. *Stroganoff Sauce for Scrambled Eggs* (Makes enough sauce for 8 portions.) Sauté 1 pound mushrooms and ½ small onion, diced, in 4 tablespoons of butter. When the mushrooms are barely cooked through, remove from the pan. Stir 2 tablespoons flour and 1 teaspoon paprika into the juices in the pan. Brown to make a roux. Add 1 cup beef broth a little at a time. Stir and cook until thickened. Turn down the flame and add ½ cup sour cream. Heat through, but do not boil. Season with salt, pepper, and Worcestershire sauce (and perhaps some dried dill) to taste. Return the mushrooms and onions to the sauce. Keep warm.
Note: You can make the entire sauce the night before. Just be careful when reheating not to let the sauce boil.

Cantaloupe Wedges (served with lime quarters and
powdered ginger to sprinkle on lightly)
Baked Eggs in Seashells*
Brioches (to buy fresh or frozen) / Butter / Jam
Coffee

Baked Eggs in Seashells

This is another wonderful way to handle a crowd of egg-
eaters. We collect large clam shells on the beach, but commercial shells (such as you'd use for a coquille) or individual baking dishes of any kind would also do. For
each serving of 2 eggs to a seashell:

1 teaspoon melted butter	Salt and pepper
2 teaspoons heavy cream	Kosher salt to hold the shells
1 teaspoon grated parmesan	steady in a large baking
cheese	pan

Swirl the melted butter around the bottom of each seashell
to coat it. Set the shells on a bed of salt in a large baking
pan. Add 1 teaspoon of cream, cheese and a dash of salt and
pepper. Break in two eggs, gently. Spoon the other teaspoon
of cream over the top, salt and pepper again. Bake in a
350° oven for 18–20 minutes, depending on how set you
like your eggs. If you prefer a runnier yolk, cover the
entire baking pan with foil.

Chilled Tomato Juice
Shirred Eggs Mongole*
No-Toaster Toast (page 46)
Coffee

This is a fine breakfast for a crowd, to slide in the oven
before you run to get dressed. Start the toast first (it will
take a little longer at the lower oven temperature you need
for the eggs). Assemble the eggs and start baking them
about 10 minutes after you start the toast.

You can make the sauce for the eggs the night before. If you do, pour it into the pan you're using for the eggs and warm briefly on top of the stove before adding the eggs.

Shirred Eggs Mongole

2 cans split pea with ham
   soup
1 cup tomato juice
½ cup heavy cream
4 tablespoons chopped onion

4 teaspoons lemon juice
Dried dillweed
2 tablespoons butter
Salt and pepper
16 eggs

Preheat oven to 300°. Using a large baking pan or, better for this quantity, the broiler pan from your oven, melt the butter in the pan on top of the stove.

Over a low flame, stir in the *undiluted* pea soup, tomato juice, cream, chopped onion and lemon juice. The sauce should be on the thick side, but thin with more cream if necessary. When warm, season to taste with dried dill, salt and pepper.

Remove the pan from the fire. Carefully break in the eggs. Bake 10–12 minutes until they are set.

To serve: Spoon out 2 eggs per serving, with some of the sauce on top. Serves 8, allowing 2 eggs per serving.

No-Menu One-Dish Filler-Uppers

> *Huevos Rancheros**
> *One-Pan Farmers' Breakfast**
> *German Apple Pancake**
> *Mouse Bites**
> *Potato Fritters**
> *Corn Cakes**

These are all filling dishes with which you don't really need to serve anything except a glass of juice first.

* Recipe follows

Huevos Rancheros

Salsa Caliente (Hot Sauce)
1 cup chili sauce
¼ cup vinegar
¼ cup brown sugar
1 tablespoon dry mustard
1 bay leaf
1 clove garlic, whole
½ teaspoon Worcestershire
    sauce

⅛ teaspoon Tabasco sauce
⅛ teaspoon crushed red
    pepper
1 tablespoon oil

8 sausages
4 pancakes

4 eggs
Butter (as needed for pan)

Make sauce by combining first group of ingredients. Let boil; turn the flame low; simmer for 1 hour. Keep the sauce hot. You can prepare the sauce in advance and reheat it. Cook the sausages and keep them warm. Use a pancake mix, or make your own. Prepare 4 pancakes 4 inches in diameter. Keep them warm on a large serving platter in low oven.

Fry the eggs, one at a time, sunnyside up. As each egg is cooked, slip it onto one of the pancakes. When each pancake has been "egged," remove the platter from the oven, pour sauce over each egg, and surround the eggs with the sausages. Serves 4.

One-Pan Farmers' Breakfast

This is a fine off-to-the-ski-slope breakfast. You can use canned ham, or leftover baked ham.

¼ cup diced onion
3 medium potatoes (cut in
    cubes, about ¾ inch)
¼ cup butter
1 can (12 oz.) chopped
    ham, cut into cubes, or
    1½ cups cubed baked
    ham

6 eggs
½ teaspoon salt
¼ cup sharp Cheddar cheese,
    shredded (you can buy
    envelopes of already
    shredded cheese)

Sauté the onion and potatoes in butter until the potatoes are lightly browned. Cover and cook 15 minutes, or until the potatoes are almost tender. Stir in the ham. Beat the eggs with salt. Pour over the potato mixture. Cook over low heat, as an omelette, occasionally slipping a spatula under the potatoes and ham to let the uncooked egg flow to the bottom. When the eggs are set, sprinkle with cheese. Cover the pan until the cheese is melted, about a minute or so. Serves 6.

German Apple Pancake

3 or 4 tart apples	2 eggs
Butter or margarine	½ cup milk
⅓ cup sugar	½ cup sifted flour
⅛ teaspoon nutmeg	¼ teaspoon salt
¼ teaspoon cinnamon	

Peel and core apples, slice thin. Cook the apples in butter five minutes. Mix sugar, nutmeg and cinnamon; add to apples. Cover and cook 10 minutes. Cool.

Mix eggs, milk, flour and salt. Beat 2 minutes. Heat 1 tablespoon butter in an ovenproof 10-inch skillet. Pour batter into pan. Add the apple mixture by spoonfuls so that it will be evenly distributed in skillet.

Bake in a very hot oven (450°) for 15 minutes. As soon as the batter puffs up in center, puncture with a fork, repeating as often as necessary. Lower heat to 350° and bake 10 minutes more. Remove from oven. (Pour 2 tablespoons butter over surface if desired.)

Serve with cinnamon—sugar to sprinkle over, if desired— and lots of sour cream. Serves 3–4.

Mouse Bites
(French Fried Miniature Pancakes)

Shari Lewis first showed me these one Sunday brunch, everybody gathered in her enormous cook-and-eat-breakfast- in kitchen. The "Mouse Bites" came from daughter Mallory who was diligently dropping batter by the teaspoonful into the frying pan. Kids love these pancakes. Just keep an eye on spattering oil. With an electric frying pan at the table, you've got a make-your-own breakfast.

Pancake batter in the amount you need: Use a Swedish pancake mix, or regular mix plus 1 tablespoon sugar for each cup of mix	Vegetable oil Powdered sugar

Heat ¾-inch oil in an electric frying pan or heavy skillet. When a drop of water sizzles in it, you're ready. Drop teaspoonfuls of batter into oil. When the "Mouse Bites" are done, they will rise to the surface. Remove them with a slotted spatula onto paper towels. Sprinkle with powdered sugar. Serve immediately, or keep warm in a low oven. They are thin and crisp and good with just the sugar, or you might try maple syrup, or sour cream, or jam.

Gordon Hyatt's Potato Fritters
(With Maple Syrup and Sour Cream)

3 medium potatoes	depending on how
1 medium onion	watery the potatoes are)
1 egg	Peanut oil to half fill a large
1 teaspoon salt	skillet
Fresh-ground black pepper	Maple syrup
Pancake flour or Bisquick (about ½ to 1 cup	Sour cream

Grate the potatoes and onion into a glass or pottery bowl. (Or you can mix the entire batter in a blender.) Beat in the egg, salt and pepper. Add enough pancake flour or Bisquick to make a thick batter. In a large skillet, heat oil. When the oil is smoking, drop the batter in by spoonfuls. Press down with the back of a wooden spoon or tablespoon to flatten each fritter slightly. Fritters are done when they are browned and rise to the top. Remove with a slotted spoon and drain on paper towels. Serve immediately with maple syrup and sour cream. Or keep warm in a low oven. Serves 4–6.

Corn Cakes

1 cup pancake mix	1 cup milk
1 cup yellow cornmeal	2 slightly beaten eggs
2 cups cream-style corn	2 tablespoons cooking oil

Stir the mix with the cornmeal. Add the rest of the ingredients. Cook on a hot griddle. Serve with maple syrup. Makes 16 four-inch pancakes.

> *Broiled Fruit**
> *Rainbow Trout**
> *Corn Bread (from a mix, follow package directions)*
> *Coffee*

Broiled Fruit

This is a quick and delicious way to serve fruit, either at breakfast or as dessert. Use an aluminum foil pan and it's even easier.

GRAPEFRUIT: Spread with honey and broil until brown.

PEACHES, PEARS, OR NECTARINES: Dip or brush with melted butter. Sprinkle with brown or white sugar. Broil until brown and glazed.

Rainbow Trout

8 trout	Salt, pepper
Flour	8 bacon strips
Cornmeal	Oil

Wipe trout with paper towels. Combine equal parts flour and cornmeal and season with salt and pepper. Dredge trout in flour mixture to coat well on both sides. Cook bacon until almost crisp, and drain. Add enough oil to bacon drippings to make ¼ inch in pan. Heat fat, but do not allow to smoke. Carefully place trout in pan and fry over medium heat 7 minutes. Gently slip spatula under fish while cooking to avoid any sticking, being careful not to break the skin. Turn fish and cook 7 minutes longer or until browned. Serves 4–8, depending on how hungry everyone is.

OUTDOOR BREAKFASTS OR BRUNCHES

Ideas for Breakfasting Outdoors

What could be more delightful than a poolside or lakeside breakfast cooked on the spot over a charcoal grill?

Bring a pan for eggs; a griddle for pancakes. Carry pancake batter in a plastic jar. Cook what you want on the grill.

1. BACON ROLLS: Warm Kaiser or French bread rolls or hot-dog buns in foil. Split, butter, and fill with cooked bacon.

2. GRILLED HAM SANDWICHES: Fry buttered buns, cut side down, in a skillet over the fire. Sauté ham slices in another skillet. Make sandwiches. Or make sandwiches first, and dip in beaten egg, then sauté on both sides.

3. PANCAKE WESTERNS: Fry pieces of bacon, chopped onion and chopped green pepper in a skillet over the barbecue until bacon is brown. Stir in beaten eggs and scramble all together. Sandwich between two buckwheat cakes (which you can make in another pan while the bacon mix is cooking).

Barbecued Brunch

Bloody Marys (see Index)
Breakfast Kebobs*
Hot buttered rolls (warm over fire in foil)
Coffee cake (warm same as rolls)
Coffee

This is a make-your-own kebob breakfast for as many people as you like. You just put out all the fixings on platters. Lots of skewers. People help themselves. (See also "Cool Pool Kebobbing," page 201.)

Breakfast Kebobs

Put out a variety of meat chunks, fruit chunks and vegetables on various platters. Guests thread their own skewers, as fancifully as they like. Keep a small pan of melted butter and a pastry brush nearby to brush with while grilling.

GOOD COMBINATIONS

1. Sausages, pineapple chunks, and mushrooms
2. Chicken livers, pineapple chunks, and bacon precooked slightly
3. Ham chunks and whole canned apricots
4. Cooked shrimp, water chestnuts, and bananas

A Make-Your-Own Omelette Brunch Buffet, Indoors or Out

White Wine, chilled
Make-Your-Own Omelettes*
Croissants / Butter / Jam
Melon Balls with Rum
Coffee

You need one or two portable cooking units if you want to cook omelettes at the buffet table. But you could do the same thing with 2 pans in your kitchen or outdoors on the grill

Make-Your-Own Omelettes

Set up a buffet table (or counter in your kitchen) with everything ready:

2 omelette pans
A large bowl of beaten eggs
  and a measure for dipping
out ¼ cup servings
Butter (for cooking the eggs)
Spatulas

A variety of accompaniments (choose from these):

A bowl of red caviar mixed
with sour cream

A bowl of chopped herbs

Sautéed mushrooms

Cooked artichoke hearts
browned in olive oil and
garlic

Curried shrimp

Each guest makes his own omelette, adding about 2 tea-spoons of any of the accompaniments just before folding the omelette. Spoon more over the top. Allow 1½–2 eggs for each guest.

Melon Balls with Rum

Use any combination of melons. Place melon balls in a large glass bowl. Spoon over orange juice with lemon juice to taste. Or use ginger ale. Add a dash of rum. Serve, garnished with mint.

Belgian Waffle Brunch Buffet

Rumdinger Punch (see index)
Belgian Waffles*
Coffee

Belgian Waffles

We first tasted these at the New York World's Fair, and, unfortunately, they've become special party breakfast in our household. "Unfortunately," because chunky people don't need Belgian waffles.

But delicious they are, and a wonderful one-dish brunch, particularly during strawberry season. For a crowd, you could bake the waffles ahead of time. Keep warm in a low oven, assemble all your materials on a buffet table, and let each one help himself.

* Recipe follows

Waffles (in the amount you need)

Sugared, sliced strawberries (Allow about ¾ cup of berries per waffle. Use frozen sliced strawberries if fresh are not available.)

Whipped cream, sweetened with a little sugar (Sorry Jean Nidetch,* but at least ¾ cup whipped cream to a waffle. Remember, 1 cup of heavy cream equals 2 cups whipped cream.)

Powdered sugar

You build your calorie castle like this:

1. Heap strawberries evenly across a hot waffle section.
2. Sprinkle generously with powdered sugar.
3. Spread whipped cream over to make a thick topping.
4. Eat any way you can. Hand-held with a large napkin underneath. Or on a plate.

* Author of *Weight Watcher's Cook Book*

SECOND-HOUSE LUNCH TIMES

. . . are nice times to give a party, or have a picnic. Otherwise, my philosophy is to breakfast big, dine well and not worry in between. (See "Weekends At a Glance," page 103).

However, since the pleasure of Second-Housing-It is flexibility, you may find yourself wanting lunch once in a while.

The two parties and menus which follow are only a small sampling of what you can do for lunch.

Please see Index for:

"Have Food, Will Travel," for travel tricks that will work for picnics.

"Stuff Kids Can Make" (chapter 9), for other sandwich ideas.

"Outdoorsmanship," where the menus are good for anytime of the day.

"Quick Appetizers."

Red, White, and Marvelous Lunch

Our neighbor and good friend, Edward Padula, produces not only Broadway shows ("Bye, Bye, Birdie"; "Red, White & Maddox"), he produces lunches as well. This was a lunch party for the cast of "Maddox" planned early that week. An all-afternoon swim-eat-and-dance-on-the-deck party for about 40 people. The crabmeat was served first, piled into individual shells Ed collects. Then came buffet lunch. Later, dessert. And always, music.

Crabmeat Salad (served on a lettuce leaf in an individual
  beach shell)
Steak Tartare Gilbert*
Cold Cut Platter
Hot Italian Garlic Bread (see Index for recipe)
Tossed Green Salad with Fruit*
Lemon French Dressing*
Chianti Wine
Fresh Fruit Compote Spiked with Kirsch
Cookies

Steak Tartare Gilbert

This is a spicy tartare (raw steak) delicious for lunch or appetizer, spread on black bread rounds.

For each pound of meat
  (top round, or sirloin,
  ground once):
2 egg yolks, beaten until
  lemony

⅓ can anchovies, mashed
  with a fork (or 1
  tablespoon anchovy
  paste)
1 small onion, chopped fine
1 tablespoon olive oil

AND TO TASTE:

Salt
Pepper
Worcestershire sauce

Dry mustard
Capers
Parsley to garnish

With two forks, or better yet, your hands, work all the ingredients into the meat. The amount of seasoning really depends on your taste. Shape the tartare into a large mound, or pile it in a bowl. Serve sprinkled with chopped parsley. 1 pound of meat will serve 3 to 4 for lunch; 6 to 8 as appetizer.

Note: Steak Tartare should be mixed and eaten almost immediately. But any leftover makes delicious cooked hamburgers the next day.

Tossed Green Salad with Fruit

The combination of fruits with greens gives this salad an unusual texture.

1½ cups grapefruit sections (canned or fresh)
2 red apples
1 cucumber
1 tablespoon fresh mint
1 head iceberg lettuce
2 heads romaine lettuce
½ head chicory
2 cups lemon French dressing below

Drain the grapefruit sections well. Core and dice the apples, but don't peel them. Slice the cucumber, also unpeeled. Tear the greens into small pieces with your hands. Toss together in a large wooden bowl. Then toss again with the lemon dressing at serving time. Serves 10–12.

Note: Fruit adds texture and flavor to many kind of green salads. Try grapes in a salad with blue cheese dressing; pears, grapefruit and avocado in a salad with garlic French dressing.

Lemon French Dressing

⅔ cup olive oil
⅓ cup fresh lemon juice
¼ teaspoon sugar
Good grind of black pepper
1–2 garlic cloves, crushed
(use, and amount, depends on your liking for garlic)
¼ teaspoon dry mustard
1 teaspoon salt

Combine all the ingredients in a jar. Cover, and shake hard until blended. Makes 1 cup dressing.

Quick, Easy, and Spontaneous Lunch

Artist Arnold Hoffman and wife, Jean, keep a larder full of basics (see chapter 2). As Jean says, "I like to wait and see what I feel like" before committing time to entertaining. And with the security of food in the house, the Hoffmans are free to pick up the phone as they feel like it. Which is what happened one rainy Sunday morning when there wasn't anything much to do. By one o'clock, we were twenty-two people at lunch.

> *Bloody Marys and Margarita Cocktails (see Index)*
> *Cheese and Crackers*
> *Spaghetti with Quick Meat Sauce**
> *Grated Parmesan Cheese*
> *Tossed Green Salad*
> *Garlic Bread*
> *Coffee and Cake*

Quick Meat Sauce for Pasta

Quick, in this case, can't mean instant. Good meat sauces just don't happen that way. The quickest thing you can do is buy ready-made meat sauce and doctor it with oregano. The recipe below, using prepared spaghetti sauce, is the quickest I know that's also passed the taste test of Italian friends.

1 pound hamburger meat	Olive oil
1 pound Italian sausage, a mixture of hot and sweet	Oregano to taste
	3 leaves fresh basil or 1 teaspoon dried basil
2 quarts prepared spaghetti sauce	2 cloves garlic, minced
	Sugar

Season the hamburger meat to your taste. Heat enough olive oil to cover the bottom of a large, heavy casserole. Brown the garlic and the sausages; then add the hamburger meat and brown. Add the prepared sauce, basil and season to taste with oregano (it will take a lot, perhaps 3 to 4 tablespoons to bring up the flavor) and a pinch of sugar. When the seasoning is right, simmer the sauce at least an hour, if you have time (30 minutes minimum). Skim off the fat from the top. Enough for 2 pounds of spaghetti, which serves 8–12, or dinner for 6 plus sauce for the freezer.

VARIATION: For an even deeper-textured meat sauce, Bolognese, add ¾ cup red wine and a package of frozen spinach before simmering.

A Salad Lunch

*Sicilian Bean Salad**
Hot Rolls
Red Wine
Fruit Basket

Sicilian Bean Salad

1 can (20 ounces) garbanzo beans (chick peas)	4 to 6 drained anchovy fillets
1 can (20 ounces) red or white kidney beans	⅓ cup salad oil (part olive oil)
1 clove garlic	2 tablespoons minced parsley
½ teaspoon salt	1 sweet red onion, thinly sliced
Pinch of crushed dried red pepper	Sausages (salami, cervelat, mortadella, galantina)
½ teaspoon marjoram	Crisp greens
⅓ cup red wine vinegar	

The day before: Drain and rinse beans in a bowl. Crush the garlic. Blend in salt, red pepper, marjoram, vinegar and anchovies. Then beat in oil. Pour over beans and refrigerate several hours.

An hour before serving, mix in the parsley and onion. Heap the salad onto a bed of greens, and arrange the sausage around edges in overlapping slices or bundles of julienne strips. Serves 6.

Soup and Sandwiches

. . . Make a hearty lunch or supper. Anything goes. Or ad lib from the recipes below.

Beer Soup with Crabmeat

If you add more crabmeat, this is a delicious quick main-dish soup, and you won't need sandwiches . . . just some hot rolls.

1 can undiluted condensed
    tomato soup
1 can undiluted condensed
    green pea soup

1 can (12-oz.) beer
1 cup milk or cream
½ pound lump crabmeat or
    1 can (6-oz.) crabmeat

Combine all the ingredients except crabmeat. Heat thoroughly without boiling. Turn off flame, stir in crabmeat and serve immediately. Also good with clams, shrimp, or scallops. Serves 4.

Spicy Tomato Soup

1 cup heavy cream
¼ cup water
1 can condensed undiluted
    tomato soup

¼ cup dry sherry
2 or 3 drops Tabasco sauce
Chopped dill or parsley to
    garnish

Add the cream and water to the can of tomato soup. Heat, but do not boil. Stir in the sherry and hot sauce. Let the soup stand to mellow in a double boiler over hot water for about 15 minutes. Serve, garnished with chopped dill or parsley (fresh or dried). Serves 4.

Blender Borscht

1 can (8¼ ounces) chopped
  beets and juice
1 cup sour cream
1 cup chicken consommé or
  instant chicken broth mix
  and water

2 tablespoons lemon juice
4 teaspoons sugar
1 teaspoon chopped dill

Blend all ingredients until smooth. Serve in chilled soup cups with one ice cube in each cup. Serves 3–4.

Corn Chowder

1 onion
3 tablespoons bacon fat or
  diced salt pork
2 cups diced raw potatoes

1½ cups boiling water
1 cup canned corn niblets
Salt and pepper
2 cups milk or light cream

Sauté onion in bacon fat or diced salt pork. Add minced potatoes and sauté until soft, but not brown. Add boiling water and corn niblets. Salt and pepper to taste. Stir in milk and heat gently. Serve with New England crackers or French herb bread.

Hashburgers

1 can (1 pound) corned beef
  hash
⅓ cup chili sauce
⅓ cup sliced stuffed olives
4 or 5 English muffins

8 to 10 slices cheese:
  American, cheddar,
  mozzarella
8 to 10 stuffed olives
Chopped parsley

Combine hash, chili sauce, olives; mix well. Split muffins; place under broiler; toast split sides lightly. Spread with hash mixture; place under broiler just long enough to heat hash slightly; then top with cheese, sliced to fit muffins. Broil just until the cheese melts. Press 1 whole olive into cheese on each muffin; sprinkle with parsley. Serve at once. Serves 8–10.

Sandwiches Stroganoff

Heat any cooked sliced meat in this quick sauce, and serve over toast. *Sauce:* Mix canned gravy with sour cream. Season with chopped onions, cooking sherry, and basil. Or make Stroganoff Sauce, page 139 (quick version, page 48).

Barbecued Pork Sandwiches

Thinly sliced cooked roast pork
1 onion, chopped
1 cup bottled barbecue sauce, or canned tomato sauce

2–3 tablespoons steak sauce (to taste)
1 tablespoon brown sugar
Salt
Butter

Sauté onion in butter until golden. Stir in barbecue sauce, steak sauce, brown sugar and salt. Taste for seasoning, then add the sliced pork and heat through. Serve over toast or hamburger buns.

Quick Sandwiches

1. SPICY GRILLED HAM 'N CHEESE: Spread bread with butter mixed with garlic salt. Lay on a slice of boiled ham, a slice of American cheese. Broil open-faced until cheese melts.

2. CUCUMBER SANDWICHES: Slice cucumbers very thin. Spread dark bread with seasoned, softened cream cheese. Lay on cucumber slices. Chopped parsley, or watercress are optional additions.

3. TUNA-AVOCADO CLUB SANDWICHES: Butter 3 slices of fresh toast. On 1 slice, spread tunafish mashed with mayonnaise and seasonings. On the second slice, spread avocado mashed with onion salt. Lay on a thin slice of tomato and lettuce if desired. Cover with the third slice. Cut in fourths diagonally, inserting a toothpick in each quarter to keep the sandwich together. Make other club sandwiches from:
Bacon, lettuce and tomato, cold sliced chicken.

4. CURRIED DEVILED EGG SANDWICHES: Make your favorite deviled egg spread, adding curry powder to taste. Spread on white bread. Lay on slices of chutney, if desired. Eat open or closed.

4

ANYTIME OF THE DAY
Eye-Openers and Closers

"Man is the only animal that drinks when he
is not thirsty."

An old saying

While cooking and eating in a second house hopefully have their appointed times, time for a drink (of something or other) can be anytime at all. And there you are feeling like a bartender or a coffee-wagon-pusher.

It need not be so. With an electric coffeepot to satisfy the perpetual coffee-breakers, and perhaps a pitcher of something put in the icebox right after breakfast, you can be prepared for the uncertainties of the day. (Also see page 218 for Drinks for Kids.)

Keeping Your Cool In General

If your household is anything like ours (be honest), the most frequent eye-hand coordinating you do is dropping ice cubes into glasses.

I won't go into the sociology of the drinking hour which these days can start at breakfast. Or the divorces over whose turn it is to mix drinks. I simply pass on to you various tricks and techniques used by people I know to get to the drinking faster.

1. *Ice cubes*

You don't have to be perpetually out of ice. Or constantly trying to get a dripping ice tray into the freezer without spilling.

Our "Tranquillity Base" is a double plastic garbage bag (one inside the other to hold the weight) that sits in the refrigerator freezing compartment and holds ice cubes.

The object of the game is to keep the plastic bag filled at all times with ice cubes which you can just reach for when needed. On a morning, or off time, empty all your ice trays at the same time into the bag. If you get in the habit of keeping the bag filled, you'll almost never run out at cocktail hour.

2. *Icing punches*

Easier than trying to buy a block of ice locally, try this: Freeze 1 or 2 large cans of fruit juice, such as pineapple juice, a day or two ahead of time. At punch serving time, open both ends of the cans. A solid block of fruit ice will drop out. Slide it into your punch bowl.

3. *About glasses*

The new plastic throwaway cups are better than paper cups for alcoholic beverages. Or, if you can't bring yourself to that, try labelling glasses with names if you're having a crowd. (I even label paper cups for teen-age parties; otherwise, they'll use dozens!) The felt-tipped pens write nicely and wash off easily. On second thought: mix them up; makes for conversation.

4. *Consider changing your serving style*

The usual cocktail protocol is to ask "what are you drinking?" which means you need to be prepared to serve any one of a dozen things.

Some friends of ours eliminate this need by deciding on one or two drinks they prepare ahead of time in pitchers. They then offer a choice of, say, martinis and Margaritas, or a pitcher of Bloody Marys. Two pitchers of hard stuff, plus a pitcher of canned fruit punch or colas for the kids can make an awfully easy afternoon's drink serving.

5. *Amounts of liquor for a crowd*

I am not going to bore you with jigger measures and their equivalents.

On hard whiskey—Scotch, bourbon, rye—figure 18 drinks to a bottle and you'll be safe. (The aficionado I live with says 12 drinks to a bottle. You decide.)

On short mixed drinks, like Margaritas, martinis, gimlets,

figure ⅓ to ½ cup mixed, per serving, depending on whether you serve over ice or not.

On tall mixed drinks, like Bloody Marys, bull shots, screwdrivers, figure 1 cup mixed, per serving.

COFFEE AND TEA REMINDERS AND RECIPES

Coffee in General

MEASURING: Use 1 coffee measure (2 level tablespoons) coffee to ¾ cup water, regardless of what kind of pot you use.

KEEPING COFFEE: Putting an opened can capped with plastic in the refrigerator will help keep coffee for about a week.

COFFEE FOR A CROWD:

For 20 servings: ½ pound coffee to 1 gallon water

For 40 servings: 1 pound coffee to 2 gallons water

To make coffee for a crowd without a large coffeepot:

In a bowl, mix 1 egg (break it and use the shell and all) with the amount of coffee you want. Add 1 cup cold water. Pour the mix into a cheesecloth bag, leaving enough room for the coffee to swell. Measure the rest of your water (less 1 cup) into a large pot. Immerse the coffee bag. Bring to a boil. Remove the pot from heat and let stand for 5 minutes. Remove the bag. Serve.

QUICK ESPRESSO IN A NON-ESPRESSO POT: Use espresso coffee. Use 1 coffee measure (or 2 tablespoons) to ½ cup water. (For a rich after-dinner coffee that's not quite as strong as all-espresso, mix equal amounts of regular and espresso coffee and use 1 coffee measure to ¾ cup water.)

ICED COFFEE:

From coffee cubes: Freeze regular coffee into cubes in your ice tray. Make iced coffee by pouring regular-strength hot coffee over the cubes.

From coffee: Brew stronger coffee (1 coffee measure to ½ cup water). Pour hot over regular ice cubes.

From instant coffee: Put 2 teaspoons instant coffee in a tall glass. Add a little warm water to dissolve. Fill the glass with ice cubes and cold water.

Tea in General

HOT TEA FOR A CROWD: Make a tea concentrate ahead of time, which you use with boiling water at serving time.

For 25 servings: Boil 1 quart of water until it has come to a full rolling boil. Pour over ⅔ cup loose tea (the equivalent of 30 teabags). Cover and let stand for 5 minutes. Stir and strain into a container.

Keep the tea concentrate at room temperature and plan to use it within 4 hours.

To serve: Pour 2 tablespoons concentrate into a cup. Fill with hot water.

Note: You can also make iced tea for a crowd this way, using 2½ tablespoons of concentrate per glass, and filling with ice cubes and water.

ICED TEA FOR 8: Boil 1 quart water. Remove from heat and add 15 teabags, or ⅓ cup loose tea. Stir, cover, and let it stand for 5 minutes. Stir again, and strain into a pitcher holding 1 quart cold water.

About iced tea: Keep your iced tea at room temperature to avoid clouding.

About instant teas: For hot or iced tea, follow the label instructions.

Hot Spiced Tea

2 quarts water
12 teabags (or use 4
    tablespoons loose tea)
½ teaspoon whole cloves

½ stick cinnamon
½ cup sugar
¼ cup lemon juice
½ cup orange juice

Bring the water to a full boil. Pour over the tea and spices. Cover, and let stand for 5 minutes.

Stir the tea and strain it. Add sugar and stir until dissolved. Add the fruit juices.

Serve immediately, or reheat without boiling. About 10 servings.

Coffee Pluses

Coffee laced with whiskey or liqueur is a lovely way to end a dinner. Use brandy, whiskey, white crème de menthe, Curaçao, kümmel, Tía Maria (for a coffee-on-coffee taste), anisette, or Cointreau.

Or make *Cappucino:* Prepare Espresso coffee. Put 2 tablespoons whipped cream in the bottom of each coffee cup. Add a dash of cinnamon. Pour hot espresso coffee over.

Danish Eggnog

This Danish version of eggnog, using coffee, is a wonderful holiday cold drink. Or an interesting dessert in itself.

6 eggs	3 cups cold strong coffee
Grated rind of 1 lemon	⅔ cup brandy or cognac
½ cup sugar	

Beat the eggs with the lemon peel until they are light and fluffy. Add the sugar, gradually, and continue to beat until thick. Slowly stir in the coffee; then brandy. Serve with a dollop of whipped cream in each cup. Makes 8–10 servings.

HARDER STUFF

Some Good Summer Vodka Drinks

The proportion in these drinks is one part vodka to three

parts liquid (or four parts, depending on how strong you like your drinks).

Bullshot: Vodka and beef bouillon; add lemon, Worcestershire sauce, salt and pepper to taste.

Screwdriver: Vodka and orange juice.

Salty Russian: Vodka and grapefruit juice. Add salt to taste.

Gimlet: Reverse the proportion. Use 1 part Rose's Lime Juice to 4 parts Vodka. (Like a martini.)

Bloody Marys, Cold and Hot

. . . are very changeable creatures. So much depends on the flavor of the tomato juice you start with, and your own taste (we like lots of lemon, for instance). The rough formula we go by is 1 part seasoned vodka to 2 parts tomato juice. (As my Aficionado says, the reason you season the vodka separately is you can tell by the color whether it's any good or not. Until you get a light brown, you ain't got enough seasoning.) If you prefer a stronger Bloody Mary, cut down the tomato juice proportion to 1½ to 1.

1 quart vodka
½ cup lemon juice (more, if you like a tastier flavor)
3 tablespoons Worcestershire sauce
1 teaspoon Tabasco sauce
Salt and fresh ground pepper
2 quarts tomato juice

Season the vodka with lemon juice, Worcestershire, Tabasco, salt and pepper in a large glass pitcher. (Add more Worcestershire if need be to make a light brown color.) Add the tomato juice. Stir hard, and taste for seasoning. Chill. Serve in a tall glass over ice cubes. (I don't like a blender for Bloody Marys because if you blend a second too long, the tomato juice separates.)

For Hot Bloody Marys

A lovely winter, apres-ski drink is the same thing, hot. Heat the tomato juice until boiling. Turn down the fire. Stir in the seasoned vodka. Taste for seasoning. Heat through, without boiling. Serve in coffee mugs. Makes 12 large servings.

Margarita

Like potato chips, you can never have just one of these knee-knocking Mexican concoctions. So the recipe below is for a pitcher full. However, you can always use the basic one-two-three formula: one part Triple Sec or Cointreau; two parts lemon or lime juice; three parts tequila.

1 cup Triple Sec or
   Cointreau
2 cups lemon or lime juice
3 cups tequila (which is
almost the entire ⅘
quart bottle, so you
might as well use it all)

Mix the ingredients in a large pitcher, and chill thoroughly. Or shake with shaved ice.

The traditional serving method is to put a little salt on your wrist. Lick the salt, swig the Margarita, and then bite into a lemon quarter.

Margarita Americano is to dip the rims of your glasses in water and then into coarse salt, then let dry.

In either case, you can pour the Margaritas, chilled, "straight up" (with no ice), or over ice cubes in each glass. The above-listed ingredients will make 12 straight-ups; 18 over ice.

Rumdinger Punch

Our good friend and publishing lady, Helen Barrow, dinged up these Rumdingers for "beach days, and before serious drinking." It's a great, easy drink for a crowd of people on a summer's day. Just watch out which way your knees bend when you get up to walk.

2 bananas
16 ounces pineapple juice
16 ounces grapefruit juice
Juice of 2 limes or lemons
16 ounces dark rum

If you have a blender, blend the bananas with some of the fruit juice until fully liquid. Or blend by hand.

Turn the banana mixture into a large bowl, or divide among two bowls if you're doubling the recipe. Stir in the rest of the ingredients. Serve over ice cubes, or cracked ice. Makes 12 punch cup servings.

Variations: Other fruit juice combinations make good Rumdingers, too. Try cranberry and grapefruit; or orange and grapefruit; or pineapple and lemon juice. Always use bananas.

Sangría

This is a lovely summery wine-and-fruit punch. The base can be bought now in most liquor stores, but it's quite simple to put together yourself.

For a party, you might want to serve sangría out of a scooped-out watermelon. Cut a thin layer, lengthwise, off the top of the melon. Scoop out all the fruit and seeds. Scallop the edges with the point of a small knife.

2 bottles (⅘ quart each)
    Burgundy or rosé wine
2 large oranges, peel and
    juice
8 lemons
6 tablespoons brandy

1 cup sugar
4 fresh peaches, peeled, and
    sliced
1 cup sliced strawberries
2 bottles (7 ounces each)
    chilled sparkling water

Peel the oranges in one long spiral strip. Pour the wine into a large container, preferably glass. Drop in the orange peel, the juice of the oranges and the juice of 6 of the lemons. Slice the remaining 2 lemons, and add. Stir in the brandy. Refrigerate several hours to blend the flavors.

About 1 hour before serving, add the sugar. Stir to dissolve. Add the peaches and strawberries. Chill again.

Just before serving, add the sparkling water. About 15 servings in wine glasses; 12 or so in punch cups.

Pineapple Paradise

4 small pineapples	2 ounces peach brandy
8 ounces pineapple juice	2 teaspoons fine sugar
2 ounces lime juice	Crushed ice
3 ounces dark rum	
2 ounces light Puerto Rican rum	

Use pineapple shells as containers for this drink. Cut the tops off pineapples about 1½ inches down. Then cut a small notch in the top through which you can insert a straw. Scoop out the interior leaving a shell about ¼ inch thick. In a shaker put the pineapple juice, lime juice, rums, peach brandy and sugar. Add crushed ice and shake. Pour into pineapples, replace pineapple tops and insert a straw in each. Serves 4.

Watermelon Sip

1 watermelon	1 cup of water
26 sprigs of fresh mint. If unavailable use dried mint	4 tablespoons powdered sugar
½ cup of rum	5th bourbon

First, cut the watermelon lengthwise so that it can hold a quart of liquid after being scooped out. Cut unequal halves; the big one makes a larger container. Scoop out the fruit. Keep the watermelon juice for an additive to the drink, if it's too strong at first taste. Put the "shell" in the refrigerator to chill. Next, in a bowl, mix the mint, rum, water and powdered sugar. Set in refrigerator to cool.

Remove the watermelon from refrigerator and fill with cracked ice. Pack the ice down. Strain the rum mixture over the cracked ice evenly. Do not get any mint on the ice. (Looks horrible if you do.) Pour the bourbon evenly over the entire concoction that is in the watermelon.

Let the mixture sit for awhile; if you drink it too soon,

it's like drinking straight bourbon. After letting it set, poke straws into the cracked ice and garnish with mint leaves. Everybody sips through his own straw. Serves 4 to 6.

Fish House Punch

This is the favorite Christmas tree-trimming brew of friends who shall remain nameless in an attempt to protect the tree, which has yet to be trimmed without being knocked over.

1 washtub   Fruit juice to taste
1 year's supply of Dregs*

When the time comes, mix all the dregs together in the washtub. Set the tub outdoors in the snow to chill. Add fruit juice if you think it's necessary. Dunk in cups and drink!

  * This requires some kind of basement storage. You simply save the dregs of bottles for a year . . . beer, wine, whiskey, rum, anything.

5

DROP-INS—"We Were Just Driving By and. . . ."

Quick, on-the-spot, sanity-in-residence solutions for unexpected guests—maybe, even, for when you're your own drop-ins.

On-the-Spot Appetizers
How to Stretch a Dinner
Main Dishes Mainly from Cans

Amy Vanderbilt and Emily Post have nothing good to say about drop-ins. But they didn't know about vacation-house living.

You've just sat down with a good book, when you hear tires crunching on the gravel. "We were driving by and thought we'd see if you're home. . . ."

Or the sun is gathering itself into a big red ball over your afternoon's sundeck party. Everybody's gone home except for three or four stragglers and now the conversation's getting interesting. You'd love to invite them to stay for dinner, but you've got half a cold chicken in the icebox you were going to nibble on later. . . .

Or you're the drop-in—you've had a late start on a Friday night, no chance to market, haven't cooked ahead, and arrive at your second house starved.

All these situations have one thing in common—they require quick-witted coping that goes far beyond mere cooking . . . new ways of rising to the occasion.

Of course you don't have to invite the drop-ins to stay. Or you can offer a drink and nothing to eat. And you don't have to open your big mouth about staying for dinner. Except it's more fun if you do. You simply need more tricks in your repertoire, which is what this chapter is all about (and which is why I was driven to write this book in the first place!).

ON-THE-SPOT APPETIZERS

(When People Drop in for a Drink)

I assume that if you imbibe in the first place, you know the value of never running out of booze, and so I assume that you will always be prepared to offer a drink to a needy drop-in. (Check Bar Supplies, listed in Index.)

It's the little things you like to nibble with a drink that can drive you up a wall.

Advance Planning

Scout your fancy food stores, or fancy food department of your supermarket for ready-to-nibbles you enjoy. Keep one or two of something on your Survival Shelf at all times. There are new products coming out constantly.

GOOD AS IS:

1. Antipastos—all kinds of pickled vegetables and mixtures in the Italian food section of your supermarket.
2. Artichoke hearts in oil
3. Cheeses—There is almost an unlimited supply of fresh and processed cheese to keep either on the shelf or in the refrigerator. The great cheeses—Brie, Camembert, Fontina, Feta, etc. should be eaten within a few days. These keep well over a longer period of time, wrapped in foil or Saran: Cream cheese, Edam, Goat cheese, Port salut, Provolone.
4. Nuts—Mixed nuts, Macadamia nuts, pistachio nuts, peanuts
5. Olives—green, black, stuffed, Greek
6. Pâté
7. Meats—salami, pepperoni, chorizo—any of the Italian and Spanish sausages will keep for weeks in the refrigerator
8. Smoked Fish—mussels, oysters, clams (toothpick and serve them)

SCOUT THE FROZEN FOOD SECTION of your market for ready-to-heat hors d'oeuvres. One package of anything in the freezer can make you a 10-minute heroine.

KEEP AT LEAST ONE ITEM FROM EACH OF THESE GROUPS ON YOUR SURVIVAL SHELF (cupboard or refrigerator).

Group 1—crackery starches to eat as is; or dip with; or get spread onto: Corn Chips, Finn crisp, Flat bread, Genoa toast, Plain bread, Potato chips, Pretzels, Ritz crackers, Soda crackers, water biscuits

Group 2—that which you spread: Canned fish—sardines, tuna, salmon, crabmeat, shrimp, herring, gefilte fish, clams.

Canned meats—Vienna sausages, liver pâtes, deviled ham, chicken, turkey. Caviar, red or black (if you can afford this, don't bother with the rest). Cream cheese, packaged dips, sour cream. Plus herbs, spices, seasonings which should be on your shelf anyway.

On-the-Spot Inventing

All right. They're here. Your advance planning is done. What happens now?

First, you look, quick, in the refrigerator and see if you have the makings for anything already on hand.

QUICK APPETIZERS FROM FOODS YOU MIGHT FIND IN YOUR REFRIGERATOR

1. Open-faced Sandwiches

Any cold meat can make an open-faced meat sandwich. Spread bread with seasoned mayonnaise (see Index for Mustard Sauce), or butter. Lay thinly sliced meat on top. Dust with parsley, black pepper. Cut into fingers, quarters, etc.

Hardboiled Egg and Herring (Anchovy): Butter bread. Top with slices of egg, add herrings or anchovies.

Tomato and Raw Onion: Spread bread with mayonnaise. Cover with a thin layer of chopped onion. Lay on very thin slices of tomato. Dust with parsley. Cut into quarters.

2. Cooked Vegetables

Bring cooked zucchini, green beans, carrots, Brussels sprouts, etc. to room temperature. Sprinkle red wine vinegar or lemon juice over to taste (which gives a vinaigrettey feel). Serve in a large bowl, each person with knives for spreading or toothpicks for spearing.

3. Leftover Artichoke and Crabmeat

Season canned crabmeat with mayonnaise, mustard, and lemon juice to taste. Put a small mound of crabmeat on individual cooked artichoke leaves. Arrange the leaves on a large tray.

4. Raw Vegetables

Cauliflower, celery, carrots, asparagus and broccoli are wonderful to serve as is with seasoned sour cream to dip in. Or try mayonnaise seasoned with anchovy paste, lemon juice and capers.

Cucumber slices can be used instead of bread or crackers and spread with seasoned cream cheese.

Cherry tomatoes covered with rock salt are good as is.

5. Leftover Swordfish—Mock Sturgeon

Cold broiled swordfish (cooked with Pacific Marinade, see Index) makes a delicious sturgeon-like appetizer. We've fooled a lot of people.

Slice the cold fish very thin. Butter thin fingers of pumpernickel bread. Lay on a slice of fish. Squeeze lemon juice and a good grind of black pepper on top.

6. Gabe's Bachelor Quickie

Put a whole cream cheese in a small bowl. Pour Worcestershire sauce over to cover. Make fork tracks along top of cheese to let sauce settle in. Serve with crackers as a help-yourself spread.

Grabbing From Your Survival Shelf

If there's nothing in the icebox, then you smile at your Survival Shelf and see what to do with what you've got. (See page 36 for how to set up a Survival Shelf.)

OFF-THE-SHELF QUICKIE APPETIZERS: Make dips, dunks and spreads by combining any of the following:

To serve cold
1. A can of chopped or minced meat with an equal part of butter. Add brandy to taste.

2. One jar Wispride cheese with a jigger of whiskey.
3. Minced clams with cream cheese and garlic.
4. Peanut butter and chutney.
5. Sour cream and chutney. Add bacon bits.
6. A jar of red caviar with sour cream and chopped onion. Use as a dip with potato chips. Or use artichoke hearts on toothpicks to dip with.
7. About ⅓ cup sour cream, ⅔ cup mayonnaise, 1 to 2 teaspoons curry powder. Use as a curry dip for potato chips or raw vegetables.

To serve hot
8. Mash sardines with butter, Tabasco sauce and lemon juice. Spread on bread fingers. Broil.
9. Wrap bacon around Waverly biscuits. Broil.
10. Canned chopped mushrooms, cream cheese and Worcestershire sauce to taste. Spread on bread. Broil.
11. Ham and cheese: spread bread with garlic butter. Lay on a slice of canned ham (or fresh). Top with any cheese you can find. Broil until the cheese melts. Cut each slice of bread into squares.
12. Quick coquilles: undiluted frozen cream of shrimp soup with sherry and paprika to taste. Heat with canned or frozen cooked shrimp, lobster chunks, scallops or crabmeat. Serve from a chafing dish; in individual shells; or over toast.

Antipasto

You can invent a large platter of antipasto in minutes, simply by arranging a variety of your canned standbys on a bed of lettuce. Serve with oil and vinegar on the side. Rolled anchovies, artichoke hearts, celery stalks (with crossed anchovy strips), cheese fingers, jars of Italian appetizers (eggplant mixes, etc.), eggs (hard-cooked and quartered), peppers, pimentoes, salami slices or cornucopia, canned tuna fish. (See Index for "Planned Ahead Appetizers.")

HOW TO STRETCH A DINNER

(When Drop-Ins Stay)

When you have unplanned guests for dinner, swallow your anxieties and try one of these methods—you will be known for your wit and competence!

1. Add to what you've already planned or
2. Make a quick new main dish from scratch

Add to What You've Already Planned

Lamb chops won't stretch. But roasts, stews, even a chicken can probably include two more. The trick is to add other things around it. (I grew up with the FHB philosophy— "family hold back"—when there wasn't enough of something for guests, the family was to keep smiling as we politely passed up the food stomachs were groaning for. But FHB can now be obsolete.) You can add a soup, salad, or dessert (following) and have a feast.

EMBRACE THE MONSTER: If your main course looks skimpy, change the whole style of the dinner. Make a buffet, using whatever you had to start with and cooking something else while you're chatting. Even a small chicken, cut up into enough pieces, can change proportion if you add a bowl of fettucine, or a vegetable casserole, a quick bread, perhaps a board of cheeses, your stretched salad, a bottle of wine and candles.

Add A Soup

A quick, doctored canned soup—or combination—put together while you're finishing the rest of the meal and served in mugs can replace a Jewish Mother. As well as start to fill up your guests.

SOME IDEAS FOR DOCTORING CANNED SOUPS

1. Follow directions on package of onion soup. Add ½ cup sherry and ½ teaspoon Worcestershire sauce. Pour into individual casseroles. Put 4 slices French bread, buttered and toasted, on top. Sprinkle heavily with grated Parmesan cheese and bake in hot oven (400°) about 15 minutes.

2. Combine green turtle soup with black bean soup in equal parts. Heat very hot, and ladle into bowls. Into each bowl, add 1 teaspoon Marsala wine and 2 teaspoons brandy. Stir gently. Garnish with chopped hardboiled egg, sliced pepperoni, and/or lemon slices.

3. Boula: Mix equal parts of pea soup and turtle soup, adding water as called for in the directions on the cans. Bring to a boil in an ovenproof casserole. Season with salt, pepper and sherry wine. Top with dabs of salted whipped cream, sprinkled with grated Parmesan. Set under your oven broiler a moment to brown. Serve immediately.

4. Chicken soup flavored with nutmeg or curry powder.

5. Tomato soup with a bay leaf or oregano; or corn, canned or fresh.

6. Black bean soup with chili powder and/or chopped onions, Cheddar cheese. Garnish with sour cream. Or corn chips. Or lace with sherry at the table. Or serve with a heap of cooked rice.

7. Substitute cream for water called for in the directions on any can of soup.

8. Lobster bisque with brandy. Serve soup good and hot; each person pours in brandy at the table.

9. Quick New England clam chowder from frozen potato soup and a can of minced clams; add water to dilute as necessary.

10. Combine tomato juice and clam broth; cream of chicken and cream of mushroom or celery; cream of celery and clam chowder; Scotch broth and consommé.

11. Canned minestrone, using vegetable juice cocktail instead of the water called for.

SOUP GARNISHES

For clear soups: Thin slices of lemon, lime, or avocado.

For cream soups: Paprika, slivers of cooked ham or chicken, grated cheese, chopped herbs (parsley, dill, chives, tarragon), sour cream, sliced olives, croutons, popcorn, crumbled bacon.

Add a Salad

You can inflate a plain tossed green salad into a course in itself by dressing it up—the salad, not the dressing. Grab some brown-and-serve rolls out of the freezer and you've got another course entirely.

Serve your salad before the main course, California style, if you're really worried about stretching the meat. Or after. Or with.

SALAD STRETCHERS:

Anchovy fillets

Canned artichoke hearts, or bottoms

Canned asparagus

Canned grapefruit, or a fresh apple (fruit makes a wonderful contrast in texture)

Canned green beans (the dilled ones are nice)

Canned hearts of palm

Canned mushrooms

Canned sliced beets, or julienne of beets

Canned zucchini

Cheese, julienned or diced

Pimiento

On-the-Spot Salad Composée with Mayonnaise Ravigote

This mixture of meats and vegetables in a spicy mayonnaise can be used as an appetizer, cold main dish or doubled or tripled as a cold meat buffet dish. It's a fine way to use up dribs and drabs of things in the icebox. You don't have to stick to every one of the ingredients.

4 slices cooked ham
4 slices cooked chicken or
   turkey
4 slices salami
6 canned beets
4 stalks celery
1 green pepper
6 pieces cocktail herring
2 apples, peeled and cored

6 canned white potatoes
8 ripe pitted olives
4 hardboiled egg yolks
Salt and pepper
1½ cups mayonnaise ravigote*
   (below)
1 Boston lettuce, shredded
   (use more lettuce if you
   need to stretch this)

Cut the ham, chicken, salami, beets, celery, green pepper, herring, apples, potatoes and olives into fine julienne strips; reserve the egg yolks to garnish with later. Combine with mayonnaise ravigote (below) and season to taste. Serve on a bed of shredded lettuce, garnished with the egg yolks, riced.

Mayonnaise Ravigote

3 tablespoons each: Capers,
   Chervil, (optional)
   Parsley, Shallots,
   (optional) Chopped
   onion
⅓ cup dry white wine

1½ tablespoons lemon juice
1½ cups mayonnaise
½ teaspoon anchovy paste
1 hardcooked egg white,
   finely chopped

In a saucepan, combine the capers, chervil, parsley, shallots and onions. Pour in the white wine and lemon juice. Simmer for 15 minutes, and strain into a mixing bowl. Cool. Beat in the mayonnaise, anchovy paste and egg white.

Add a Doctored Vegetable

1. Boil the juice from any canned vegetable with ¼ onion, grated, a dash of sugar and salt. Add the vegetables and cook fast, just to heat through.
2. Sprinkle buttered bread crumbs on *asparagus, broccoli, cauliflower.*
3. Canned cheese sauce can be heated to top *cauliflower.*

* Recipe follows

4. Mix canned onions, drained, with canned cream of celery soup, undiluted; plus ½ cup cream for *quick creamed onions*. Season to taste.
5. *Bean Panache*. Cook frozen lima beans and green beans according to package instructions. Toss together with melted butter and bread crumbs.
6. Arrange *canned tomatoes* in a baking dish. Top with a mixture of ½ cup breadcrumbs, 1 teaspoon oregano, salt, pepper, chopped parsley, 1 tablespoon lemon juice and 4 tablespoons butter. Brown under a low broiler.
7. *Curried bean sprouts*. Combine 1 can bean sprouts (1 pound) with 1 can French style green beans, drained (15½ ounces) in a shallow baking dish. Heat 1 can condensed undiluted cheese soup with curry powder to taste (1 teaspoon or more). Stir in ¼ cup sour cream. Pour over beans. Bake 20 minutes at 400°. Serves 6.

Add a Dessert

BRINGING DESSERT WITH YOU

With all the bakeries and patisseries in the cities, and local doughnut shops along the highways, dessert is the easiest food to buy and carry. We have a neighbor, down the road from us, in Bridgehampton, who runs a "Two O'Clock Bakery." If you go by at two in the afternoon, you can pick up warm breads and cakes, brownies, and cookies.

You won't compromise your ego if you run down the road once in awhile, or drive a cake out for a party.

SURVIVAL SHELF DESSERTS

With a freezer, you can keep one or two dessert standbys, such as:

1. Ice cream: plain, rolls, sherbet, etc.
2. Frozen cakes (I wouldn't bake a banana cake after tasting Sara Lee's)
3. Frozen pies, ready to bake, or already baked.
4. Something you've made ahead of time.

But even without a freezer, there are choices, albeit for simple things. Aside from the several thousand packaged cookies starching up the supermarkets, there are ready-to-serve canned desserts put out by specialty canners such as S.S. Pierce—puddings, Babas au rhum, etc.—expensive, but a solution; and canned fruits, which can be doctored up to a point. And of course, all the mixes for cakes and puddings if you have time.

ON-THE-SPOT INVENTING

Luckily, dessert is not much of a problem these days, unless you've never heard of weight watching. So chances are you won't need to worry. Just serve what you had. Or

Add a bowl of fresh fruit
Add ice cream to à la mode a pie, cake, pudding or brownies
Add cookies to go with a fruit dessert. (I always try to keep a tin of fancy cookies, such as Italian macaroons, on the Survival Shelf.

DESSERTS FROM CANS

1. Canned date nut bread, warmed, sliced and spread with cream cheese.
2. Fruit compote (from any canned fruit or combination): Boil up the syrup with an equal amount of wine, a cinnamon stick, and lemon juice to taste. Pour over fruit. Refrigerate until good and cold. (Put in your ice-cube section for quick chilling.)
3. Mandarin oranges mixed with sliced ginger and lichee nuts (if available).
4. Figs stuffed with almonds.
5. Guavas served with softened cream cheese and sesame crackers (Brazilian favorite), or plain Saltines.
6. Pineapple tidbits and orange sections, marinated in ginger ale.
7. Quick Cherries Flambées—Heat canned bing cherries in their juice. For 4 servings, add 4 tablespoons warm brandy. Light with a match to flambé. Spoon over ice cream.

8. Broiled canned fruit—Put canned peaches or pears cup-side up in a shallow baking dish. Put ½ teaspoon honey, brown sugar or maple syrup and a good squeeze of lime juice into each hollow. Pour rum over the fruit. Heat 15 minutes at 300°. Before serving, baste with rum, and run under the broiler for 2 minutes.

OTHER QUICK DESSERTS

A-la-mode—With ice cream you can à la mode cake, pie, cookies, doughnuts, fruit, pudding. Try a watermelon disc with pistachio ice cream on top.

Ambrosia—Pour a little curaçao (or any orange liqueur) over sugared orange and banana slices. Add a package of grated coconut. Chill.

Broiled grapefruit—broiled with honey and rum.

Chantilly—Any fruit (berries or bananas for example) folded into whipped cream (flavored, if you like, with kirsch or Cointreau) is elegant.

Cheese and bread or crackers (with or without fresh fruit)— It's well worth a special trip to a cheese store to keep some of the better cheeses around for dessert. Super-markets simply don't carry the great dessert cheeses such as Gourmandise, Triple crème, Brie, Camembert (al-though their Liedercranz is good).

Custard (from a mix) with maple syrup.

Doughnuts with chocolate sauce.

Fruits in liqueurs—Pass your favorite liqueur to spoon over sliced, sugared fresh fruit.

Quick whips—Fold any kind of junior baby fruit (1 jar) into 1 cup of heavy cream, whipped. Add lemon juice to taste. Serve as is, or with whole fruit slices on top. (Peaches on peaches; prunes on prunes; etc.)

Ricotta cheese—With a fork, mash in ground espresso coffee (about a teaspoon) and sugar to taste. A very unusual Italian dessert, good served with grapes.

Sour cream on fruit—Blueberries, peaches, and strawberries are fine just sugared with sour cream on top.

MAIN DISHES MAINLY FROM CANS

This is not as hard as it sounds, but it does depend on a certain attitude from you plus some help from your refrigerator. No apologies, or you'll ruin the ambience of spontaneous entertaining.

I once, in a fit of good will and probably one Rumdinger too many, invited eleven people to stay after afternoon sundecking. As friends helped set the table and clear up the afternoon's mess, I hastily concocted a salad composée (page 87), using everything I could lay my hands on from the icebox and cupboard. Quick mayonnaise-sour cream dressing. Augmented by quick ready-to-bake refrigerator biscuits, fruit and cookies. Not a great dinner, but it worked. And we had fun, which is what really counts.

First of all, drag out some appetizers (if you haven't already) to keep people busy while you're inventing, and, hopefully, to take the edge off their appetites, and then get busy. . . .

Survival Kits

These are the main dishes, the main ingredients of which we call our "Survival Kits," because you can store them ahead of time and be prepared (see page 36). These ingredients in the recipes are arranged so you can quickly see what to shop for ahead of time. The rest of the ingredients are generally staples and herbs you would have on hand. However, glance over the recipe. If chili powder or saffron aren't the kinds of condiments you ordinarily keep, buy them when you assemble the Kit.

Bouillabaisse

If this isn't exactly what French fishermen's wives do, why don't let it bother you one bit. It's what *you* do.

From your survival kit

1 can (16-ounce) Italian tomatoes

1 can (10½-ounce) minced clams

1 large can (16-ounce) tuna or salmon

1 can (8-ounce) oysters or mussels

1 can (4½-ounce) tiny shrimp

1 can (7¾-ounce) lobster or crabmeat

1 loaf French bread or reasonable facsimile to dunk with

Plus

1 large onion, chopped

3 green onions, chopped (optional)

1 clove garlic, minced

2 tablespoons cooking oil

1 bay leaf

Pinch of saffron

Oregano (to taste)

Minced parsley

½ cup dry white wine (optional, but it doesn't taste as good without it)

1 to 2 tablespoons lemon juice to taste

Salt and pepper

Open all the cans. Brown the onions and garlic in oil. Add the tomatoes, 1 cup water, plus the juices from the cans of seafoods. Stir in bay leaf, oregano, and parsley and simmer, covered, for 15 minutes. Add wine. Now turn off heat and gently stir in all the seafood and saffron. The trick is to not let any of the fish boil . . . or even cook . . . since this toughens them. However, if your husband likes scalding liquids, ignore my advice and bring everything back to simmer point. Season to taste with salt, pepper and lemon juice. Serve in large bowls with heated French bread for dunking. Serves 6–8.

Variation: If you have time, add a quick *Aïoli* sauce which, if you add a dash of grated orange peel, actually turns the soup into a "bourride." And since no self-respecting

Frenchman would use the canned fish anyway, why not improvise all the way. The taste is delicious!

Quick Aioli sauce: Add 3 or 4 cloves of crushed garlic and an egg yolk to a cup of mayonnaise. Stir 1 tablespoon into the soup before you serve. Serve the rest of the sauce on the side. Put a dollop into the soup when eating.

Chicken à la King

With a can of boned chicken on the shelf, you've got the makings of a number of à-la-kingy quickies.

From your survival kit

1 can or jar (13-ounce) boned chicken

1 can (4-ounce) sliced mushrooms

1 small jar roasted pimentoes (optional)

Something to serve it over: hot rice, wild rice, waffles, English muffins, biscuits, patty shells

Plus

3 cups liquid (which can be a mix of milk, cream, the juices from the canned chicken, the liquid from the mushrooms, chicken broth. Or use half milk and half chicken broth)

4 tablespoons butter

Onion salt

4 tablespoons flour

Salt, pepper and paprika to season

Sherry wine or Madeira wine to flavor

Open the cans of chicken and mushrooms, drain off liquids, and add the other liquids to make 3 cups. Heat in saucepan, then pour back into measuring bowl and keep hot. In the same saucepan, melt the butter and add a dash of onion salt. Gradually add the flour, stir over a low flame for 3 to 5 minutes to make a roux. Gradually add the hot liquid, stirring constantly to blend well. Stir until the sauce thickens. Season to taste with salt, pepper, paprika, and a tablespoon or two of wine. (Or practice instant saucery by adding these same seasonings to canned white sauce; heat and use as directed below.)

For Chicken à la king, cut the canned chicken into small pieces. Add to hot sauce along with the sliced mushrooms and 3 tablespoons chopped pimento. Check the seasonings and add more to taste. Serve hot mixtures over toast or any of the underpinnings listed above. Serves 4.

For Curried Chicken à la king, add 1 to 2 teaspoons curry powder (or more if you like a hotter curry) along with the flour when making the sauce. Sprinkle almonds on top, or serve with chopped peanuts.

With ham: Use diced cooked ham and half the amount of chicken. Madeira wine in the sauce is delicious.

With minced clams: Use minced clams and half the amount of chicken. Use white wine to flavor the cream sauce.

Baked à la King: Turn the finished à la King into a greased casserole dish. Sprinkle with buttered crumbs and Parmesan cheese. Heat in a 400° oven until the top is brown.

Chili Pie

From your survival kit

2 cans (15 ounces each) chili con carne with beans	6 slices American cheese (the sliced and wrapped variety will keep a few weeks unopened, or tightly rewrapped, in your refrigerator)
2 cans (4 ounces each) Vienna sausages	
24 soda crackers	

Plus

2 cloves garlic, crushed	1 tablespoon paprika
1 teaspoon cumin seed	

Heat, but don't boil the chili. Add the seasonings. Slice the sausages and stir them into the chili. Crumble the crackers and stir them in. Pour into an ovenproof casserole. Top with cheese slices. Heat at 350° until the cheese melts. Serve sprinkled with more cracker crumbs, and chopped onion, if you like. Serves 6.

Creamy Chipped Beef

From your survival kit

4 ounces chipped or dried
    beef
1 can (14½ ounces)
    evaporated milk
Package instant mashed
    potato flakes (of which
    you need 1 cup)

Bread, soda crackers or
    muffins (for base)

Plus

3 tablespoons instant minced
    onion

2 tablespoons butter
Pepper

Chop the chipped beef. Brown it lightly in butter in a medium saucepan. Add 1½ cups water, the undiluted evaporated milk, onion, and pepper to taste. Bring to a boil. Stir in potato flakes and mix until creamy. Serve immediately over toasted bread, English muffins, or crackers. Serves 3–4.

Chop Suey Casserole

From your survival kit

½ lb. package medium wide
    noodles, cooked
1 can (10½-ounce) cream of
    mushroom soup,
    condensed, undiluted
1 can (16-ounce) chop suey
    vegetables, drained

1½ cups diced cooked
    chicken (from can or
    freezer)
½ cup canned French-fried
    onions or chow mein
    noodles

Plus

½ cup water

1 to 2 tablespoons soy sauce

Cook the noodles as directed on package. In a 1½-quart casserole, mix all the ingredients except the French fried onions. Bake at 375° for 25 minutes. Top with onions. Bake

5 minutes more. (Or leave out the noodles; heat meat, vegetables and soup in a double boiler and serve over rice.) Serves 4–6.

Corned Beef Patties

From your survival kit

1 can (12 ounces) corned beef	1 package instant mashed potatoes

Plus

1 egg, beaten	Butter or margarine for the
3 tablespoons instant minced onion	mashed potatoes
	Salt and pepper
2 tablespoons butter or oil (for frying)	Parsley flakes

Make 4 cups instant mashed potatoes, using the water, but *omitting* the milk called for in the package instructions. (So the potatoes will be thick enough to bind the corned beef.) Shred the corned beef with a fork. Stir it into the potatoes with the egg and onion. Season to taste with salt, pepper and parsley flakes. Divide the mix into 8 mounds and shape each into a thick patty. Sauté in butter, turning once, until crusty brown. Serves 4.

Presto Pesto
(Noodles With Seafood Sauce)

With apologies to the classic Italian pesto—a cool mix of garlic, basil and oil pounded by pestle, and a nice substitute for the RAF arm lifts—this is a quick hot adaptation, using the same flavors, that has become one of our regular Survival Kit dinners. We cheated on the fresh basil, because we keep some in the kitchen herb garden. On the particular late, tired Friday night this got invented, we just ran out and cut some. But dried basil will do, too.

From your survival kit

1 can (6½-ounce) crabmeat
1 can (4½-ounce) baby
   shrimp

1 pound fettucine, or any
   wide egg noodle

Plus

¼ pound butter
¼ cup olive oil
1 onion, chopped
5 cloves garlic
5 fresh basil leaves, minced
   with scissors (or 2

tablespoons dried, soaked
   in warm water)
Salt and fresh ground pepper
¼ cup white wine (optional)
Fresh grated Parmesan or
   Romano cheese

Pick over the crabmeat to remove membranes, drain it and the baby shrimp, saving the juices.

Melt the butter with the olive oil. Sauté the chopped onion and garlic until they are golden. Add basil, salt, pepper, wine, and the juices from the cans of seafood. Let simmer over very low heat. Stir in seafood just before serving. Taste for seasoning.

Meanwhile cook the fettucine according to package directions. When the noodles are *al dente,* drain them and arrange on a large platter. Pour the Seafood Presto Pesto over. Serve with freshly grated cheese on the side. Serves 4.

Ragout de Boeuf Bourguignon

From your survival kit

2 cans (1½ pounds each)
   beef stew

Optional: 1 package
   refrigerator biscuits or 1
   package instant mashed
   potatoes

Plus

1 clove garlic, minced
½ teaspoon thyme
1 bay leaf
2 teaspoons soy sauce

6 tablespoons chili sauce
1 tablespoon parsley flakes
½ cup Burgundy wine
Parmesan cheese (optional)

Simmer the stew with garlic, thyme, bay leaf, soy sauce, chili sauce, parsley and wine for 10 minutes.

To serve with biscuits: Pour the hot stew into a casserole. Top with 10 refrigerator biscuits. Sprinkle the biscuits with additional parsley flakes. Bake at 400° 15–20 minutes, or until the biscuits are done. The stew has to be hot to begin with or the bottoms of the biscuits won't get done.

To serve with potatoes: Prepare instant mashed potatoes. Pour the stew into a casserole. Top with the potatoes. Sprinkle with Parmesan cheese. Dot with butter. Bake until browned. Serves 6.

Baked Spaghetti

This is easy because you don't have to cook the spaghetti first. Just toss it in with everything else.

From your survival kit

2 cans (8 ounces each) tomato sauce
½ pound spaghetti
1 can prepared meatballs (or ½ pound chopped beef from your freezer)
1 small jar pitted black olives

Plus

2 slices bacon, diced
2 medium onions, chopped
1 clove garlic, minced
1½ teaspoons salt
Pepper to taste
1 teaspoon chili powder
2½ cups water
1 cup grated Cheddar cheese

Fry the bacon about 2 minutes. Add onions and garlic. Cook until soft. If you're using ground meat, add it now and cook until browned. If you're using meatballs, break them into small chunks with a fork. Add meat, salt, pepper, chili powder, tomato sauce and water. Cover and simmer 25 minutes. Stir in the olives, sliced.

Into a greased 2-quart casserole, build up layers as follows: half the uncooked spaghetti broken into pieces, half the sauce, half the cheese; repeat the layers.

Cover and bake in a 350° oven, 30 minutes. Uncover and bake 15 minutes longer, or until browned and bubbly. Serves 4–5.

Tamale Pie

From your survival kit

1 can tamales
1 can chili con carne
1 can (12 ounces) whole
   kernel corn, drained

1 can pitted pimento-stuffed
   olives (whatever size you
   want to contribute to
   this venture)

Plus

Grated cheese
Chili powder to your taste

1 clove garlic, crushed
½ teaspoon cumin seed

Slice each tamale into 4 pieces. Mix the chili and the corn with chili powder, garlic, cumin seed (to your taste). In a greased casserole, make a layer of tamales and a layer of chili repeating until you've used the ingredients. Sprinkle sliced olives on top. Heat in a 350° oven about 20 minutes, or until well heated through. Just before serving, sprinkle with grated cheese. Put under broiler until the cheese melts. Serves 4.

6

WEEKENDS, WITH OR WITHOUT HOUSEGUESTS

Or, why should everyone have a vacation except you?

"Fish and visitors stink after three days."

Benjamin Franklin

It's Friday, thank God, and all the television weathermen at once, for once, are predicting clear skies, and the family's going to be *together* for the whole lovely weekend, and all you are responsible for are seven meals (or four or five, depending on what you can get away with) in between swimming, tennis, partying, and dishwashing.

That's only the rough sketch of a weekend for most of us. Color in other possibilities such as weekend house guests; friends in the neighborhood you'd like to see for a drink; perhaps a party that's on *you* . . . and it becomes apparent that a little philosophy and a *lot of planning* are needed to keep you out of bed on Monday morning.

First a little bit of philosophy: A weekend is work, but it can be less work if you'll let it be.

Plan Your Weekend Style

Unless you're planning a gourmet weekend, with everybody in the kitchen experimenting and salivating from meal to meal, your big problem is planning the menus and cooking time so *you* have time to have fun, with or without guests.

The best formula I can suggest is an either-or one. Either you try to get as much cooking as possible out of the way before the weekend starts, or you plan menus that can be done easily at the last minute. Anything in-between is weekend suicide.

Your Weekend Style

Even before you get to the planning of a specific weekend menu, it's a good idea to put a picture into your head of a weekend style which works for you. Here's where you make your decisions about three meals versus two for Saturday; what time dinner or supper on Sunday; are people coming for drinks, etc., bearing in mind that your style may shift from weekend to weekend, as ours usually does depending on the guests and the traffic.

Here's a rundown of the kinds of choices to think about:

Weekends at a Glance

Cocktails at any time

Get a rough idea of whether or not you'll be having people for drinks. Prepare accordingly.

See "Anytime of the Day" for drink-handling ideas.
See "On-The-Spot Appetizers" for quickies.
See "Planned Ahead Appetizers" following.

Friday Nights

Simple dinners.

Saturdays

Saturday Breakfast: Nothing fancy. Bacon and eggs, toast or rolls. Juice, milk, coffee.

Saturday during the day: I really am for no lunches, or else you'll be in the kitchen all day. We often indicate that snacks are in the icebox. Anybody who gets hungry can help himself (and put away any dishes he uses).

Snacks

A chunk of salami or bologna, sausages, sliced meat
Cheeses
Individual shrimp cocktails (from the frozen food section of your market)
Herring in cream sauce
Bread, rolls
A pitcher of iced tea (kept out of the icebox and iced as you pour it) or a pitcher of lemonade
Soft drinks
Milk

If you find that you can't go for the no-lunch plan, nor convince yourself it suits weight watchers just fine, then plan ahead, or make something right after breakfast, and set out a buffet in the early afternoon. Use paper plates and cups.

Lunch buffet

A platter of sandwiches or a bowl full of tuna fish salad, or egg salad, or (more elegant) crabmeat salad. Put a tray of bread alongside, butter and mayonnaise. Everyone helps himself. Or a ratatouille or a chef's salad (just tossed salad with any bits of meat and cheese you have around. Nice with Russian dressing) or a hot soup.
Fruit
Cookies or cake; or a platter of doughnuts
Drinks

Saturday night

The big meal of the weekend. Here's where planning early in the week can help enormously.

You may decide to cook ahead.

You may decide to cook more of something in order to have it again for Sunday.

You may decide to barbecue, or have a picnic, or build a fire on the beach. Or, if it's bad weather, maybe you'll want to experiment with a new dish on Saturday afternoon, letting everybody help.

Sundays

Sunday breakfast

We usually like to make this meal a brunch, and the big meal of the day. It's pancake or waffle time. Or Eggs Stroganoff. Or Huevos Rancheros (see Index).

On a beautiful morning, it's delightful to brunch outdoors. If you own one of those new propane-fueled portable cooking devices, you might consider cooking by the pool or lake; if the patio's got an electrical outlet, you can plug in an electric skillet.

The rest of Sunday

. . . depends on when your guests, if you have them, are leaving, and whether or not it's the end of the weekend for you, too. What you need is a minuteman approach. A mental framework that allows you to be ready for anything.

Late lunch. A three o'clock lunch works fine for people facing a long drive who don't still want to be driving on Monday.

Early dinner. Dinner at five or six lets you have the afternoon doing whatever it is you want to do and still get you or your guests on the road at a reasonable hour.

Light breakfast—midday dinner. It's very American and traditional to have a roast chicken-mashed-potatoes-and-gravy dinner Sunday midday. I like it too—but only in bad weather or winter. Because I can't figure out how the lady of the house gets out of the kitchen with this menu. But if you like your kitchen that much, go ahead. Or cook ahead.

Sunday supper. With a big noon brunch and no driving pressures, a fun supper can be your option—hot sandwiches, chili, spaghetti, pizza. Also there's a Near East dish, new to this country, called Falafel. This is a spicy mix of dried chick-peas which you can buy now at many specialty stores. Along with it, you buy an eastern flat bread called "pita" or "Sahara bread." The chick peas are cooked in patties, like hamburgers, stuffed into a pocket in the pita, and eaten like a taco.

The Care and Training of Houseguests

Well, of course you want to have Joan and David out. And what about Bobbie and Bert? Or Bill and Janou? That's what the house is for, isn't it? And don't forget the children's friends . . . John and Daniel and Larry and Gail and Janie and . . . unless you have servants who will meet your guests at the train in Southampton (I always press my nose against the cracked glass of the Long Island Railroad in sheer disbelief as the Rollses roll up) heed this second little bit of philosophy: Guests can be trained. (Or put back on the train!)

When You're Inviting Guests

. . . be clear and explicit about when you expect your friends to arrive and leave. Yes, *leave.* Or you may find yourself sitting around Sunday wondering when in God's name they're clearing out and do you have to cook another meal.

In a less Amy Vanderbilty tone, I suggest a few alternate scripts, such as these:

(Precisely): "Will you come up after lunch, Saturday, and stay through Sunday supper?"

(Evasively): "Come up Friday night. You'd better plan to grab a bite on the way because you can't tell about the traffic. And if you plan to leave midday, Sunday, you'll beat the jams."

(Magnanimously): "Come out Friday whenever you can. Don't worry about traffic, we'll wait dinner for you. Can you stay until Monday morning?"

When Guests Invite Themselves

. . . which people have a habit of doing the minute they know you've got a vacation house, be prepared to be realistic, be firm, and don't let yourself be imposed upon. Most of my over-thirty generation suffers needless guilt about accommodating other people's brass. Tell them you're taking a second honeymoon for a few weekends; or you wish you could have them up only you can't; or make plans. But be good to yourself!

Telling Guests What To Bring

While you're inviting, be sure to mention any special clothing that might be needed. A club dance, a berry-picking picnic, a windy October all require something special. And should you have bedding problems for one reason or another, there's really nothing wrong in asking close friends—the only kind you invite when you have bedding problems!— to bring an extra blanket.

House Rules

After Bill, and Susan, and George and Sally arrive (and they have a lovely clean place to sleep, with a book, facial tissues, ashtray, and as somebody has suggested, candles—for emergencies—nearby), let them know your house rules and routine.

What time for breakfast? Or not to worry about what time breakfast. (See "Coping With Breakfast Time," page 44.) Do you expect guests to make their own beds? (On Sundays, I usually ask guests to strip their beds and give me the sheets. Unless they're staying over till Monday.)

Does your house have any particular foibles? We have bathroom fans, for instance, that have to be turned on every time one showers. This little fact gets worked in during the "house tour" we always give, shortly after arrival.

Let guests help you. The ability to delegate responsibility is the mark of minor genius in any household. Is there any reason (assuming of course you're not the one with the Rolls I saw in Southampton) you can't have table-setting, sauce-stirring, fire-starting help? Just ask.

Planned Ahead Appetizers

If you're dreaming of a long weekend catching up with old friends over cocktails, plan an appetizer to have ready when you want it.

Here are a few of our favorites.

Marinated Mushrooms

36 small mushroom caps	2 tablespoons sugar
2 tablespoons soy sauce	1 teaspoon salt
4 tablespoons vinegar	½ cup minced onions
3 tablespoons sherry	

Wash, dry, and peel the mushrooms. Combine the soy sauce, vinegar, sherry, sugar, salt and onions in a saucepan. Bring to a boil and pour over the mushrooms. Marinate for 24 hours. Drain and serve on cocktail picks. These will keep for a week. Take out the ones you need and leave the others in the marinade.

Sweet and Sour Meatballs

If you're having a long cocktail hour with a light or late dinner, try these Chinese meatballs. Plunk your pan on the table and give everybody toothpicks to fish with. If that's too casual, use a keep-warm dish or tray. These also make a good hot dish for buffet dinner.

2 pounds chopped beef	1 bottle Heinz chili sauce
5 ounces (or half the 10-ounce jar) Welch's grape jelly	1 lemon
	Salt, pepper

In the morning: Season the hamburger with salt and pepper. Form into tiny meatballs. Refrigerate. (You can also freeze up to a month ahead of time.)

Prepare the sauce: Melt the jelly in a pan over a low flame. Add chili sauce and lemon juice to taste. Simmer until well blended.

45 minutes before serving: Drop the meatballs into the sauce. Cover. Simmer. Serve in the sauce with toothpicks on the side to dunk with. Makes 32–36 meatballs.

Bacon and Egg Dip

Ahead of time: Hardboil and mash eggs with dried mustard, onion, salt, pepper, and mayonnaise to taste. Fry bacon strips (1 for every egg) until very crisp.

At serving time: Crumble the bacon and stir through the eggs with a fork. Serve with potato chips to dip with or rye bread squares to spread on.

Mini-Burgers

One of our friends likes this so much, she always keeps a pound of hamburger meat in the freezer to have ready.

Have ready: Hamburger meat, seasoned to your taste. (1 lb. will make 18-20 mini-burgers.)

At serving time: Spread melba toast rounds (or try the new onion-flavored or cheese-flavored toasts) with ketchup or mustard. Spread on a *thin* layer of seasoned hamburger meat. Pop under the broiler to brown quickly, about 1 minute. It's the thin layer of meat contrasted with the crisp melba that gives this its goodness.

Wedges

Ahead of time: Spread spicy cream cheese (cream cheese mixed with horseradish, or with onions and Worcestershire sauce) on 5 slices of bologna or salami. Stack the meat slices on top of each other, putting the top one spread-side down. Wrap in wax paper. Refrigerate.

At serving time: Cut into individual wedges, securing each one with a toothpick.

Shrimp and Artichoke Buffet

Have on hand: Cooked shrimp; canned artichoke hearts; Russian dressing; a large cabbage with the center hollowed out enough to hold a small bowl.

At serving time: Put the Russian dressing in the small bowl that fits into the cabbage. Spear shrimp and artichoke hearts separately on toothpicks. Insert the toothpicks all around the cabbage.

For other good planned-ahead appetizers in this book, see Index for recipes.

Weekend Dinner Menus to Vacation By

The menus which follow are planned to give you a maximum amount of time *out* of the kitchen, or let you cluster your cooking ahead of time. Some are easier than others. Please mix and match the menus and scatter them over a weekend among the obvious American favorites for which I am not giving you recipes—plain hamburgers, hotdogs, barbecued steak and chicken; corn on the cob; strawberry shortcake, and all the wonderful summer fresh fruits and vegetables. The old standbys are great. It's just that once in awhile you don't want to hear, "What? Corn again?"

Check the "No-Menu End-of-the-Weekend Leftover Recipes" at the end of this chapter for some Sunday-savers.

Consider some of the brunch recipes in Chapter 3 as potential suppers, too.

TO ROAST AHEAD . . . OR NOT

*Italian Roast Beef**
Spaghettini tossed with butter and grated cheese
*Zucchini and Mushroom Salad**
*Orange Oranges**
Coffee

When To Cook:

Italian Roast Beef takes about an hour before dinner. Or cook it ahead for only half an hour and refrigerate or freeze. Bring to room temperature before reheating for about half an hour.

Spaghettini can be made just before dinner.

Zucchini and Mushroom Salad—make in the morning and serve chilled.

Orange Oranges—make in the morning.

Italian Roast Beef

⅛ pound (½ stick) butter
4-pound eye of the round roast
1 onion, peeled and sliced
Salt
Pepper
Nutmeg
1 tablespoon grated Romano cheese

1 cup dry vermouth
3 tablespoons chopped fresh parsley
1 teaspoon chopped lemon rind
1 clove garlic peeled and chopped
1 teaspoon anchovy paste

Melt half of the butter in a low flameproof casserole and lightly brown the meat and onion. Season meat with salt, pepper, and nutmeg. Sprinkle grated cheese over all. Roast uncovered at 350°, about 40 minutes for rare beef. Baste now and then with half the vermouth.

Just before serving, add a mixture of parsley, lemon rind, garlic, anchovy paste, rest of the butter and vermouth to the juices in the pan. Serve separately as sauce. Serves 6 to 8.

Zucchini and Mushroom Salad

Raw young zucchini, washed and sliced thin, may be added to any kind of green salad to add texture and taste. But try this too:

2 small zucchini
Olive oil: 1 tablespoon for sautéing and ¼ cup for dressing
½ pound fresh mushrooms
1 teaspoon wine vinegar

¼ teaspoon salt
1 teaspoon sour cream
½ teaspoon prepared mustard
1 head romaine lettuce (not too large)
1 head Boston lettuce

Wash the zucchini, trim off the stem ends and slice into very thin unpeeled rounds. Sauté as follows: Heat a heavy frying pan. When a drop of water sizzles on it, add 1 tablespoon olive oil and heat. Add the zucchini. Sauté at high heat for one minute, turn down the heat, cover, and steam over low heat for 4–5 minutes.

The zucchini should still be crisp.

Wipe the mushrooms, trim off the tough bottom of the stems. Slice them down through the caps and stems into thin slices. Combine the sautéed zucchini, the pan juices, and the mushroom in a bowl.

Marinate the vegetables in the refrigerator all day (or at least two hours); mix the remaining olive oil, vinegar, salt, sour cream and mustard. Pour over vegetables and stir to blend.

Just before serving: Line a salad bowl with the greens, washed, dried and crisped. Turn in the zucchini, mushrooms and all the dressing. Toss lightly. Serves 6.

Orange Oranges

Cut a lid from the tops of oranges. Scoop out the fruit. Pack the orange shells with orange sherbet. Put the lids back on. Wrap each orange in foil, and freeze until serving time.

> *Rump Roast of Beef* *
> *Potatoes, Carrots and Onions Cooked with the Beef*
> *Tossed Green Salad with Fruit* (see Index)
> *Chocolate Mousse* *
> *Coffee*

Ruth Ellen Church (the well-known Mary Meade of the Chicago *Tribune*) has been driving 200 miles to her farm "almost every weekend in summer . . . using the place in winter as a winter sports lodge. For weekends of fun, I try to carry most supplies from home in Chicago. Frozen ahead, ready to heat and eat."

This cook-and-carry style is a large part of the repertoire of almost every weekender I know. As Mrs. Church says, "I don't want to be stuck in the kitchen while everyone else has fun."

When To Cook:

Make the *rump roast* in your first house to carry to your second; or extract one meal from it in your first house, freeze the rest and carry to your second; or cook in your second house and freeze half for another time. It's this kind of flexibility that gives you time for fun.

The *mousse* can be made the same day, or up to 3 days ahead.

Rump Roast of Beef

10-pound rolled rump of beef	3 large onions
Salt and pepper	1 stalk celery with leaves
Oil or drippings for browning	1 bay leaf
½ lemon	Water, stock (1 cup or more)
2 cloves garlic (optional)	Red wine (optional)

Rub the roast with salt and pepper and brown it well on all sides in a heavy pot or Dutch oven that has a close-fitting lid. Put the lemon in the pot. Garlic may be cooked part time with the meat and then removed, or, if you like garlic, put the cloves through a garlic press and add them in this form. Place onions and celery in the pot, add the bay leaf, 1 cup water or beef bouillon or stock, then cover tightly and cook very slowly until the meat is fork-tender, 3½ to 4 hours. If you wish to add wine, add as much as a cupful along the way. If liquid cooks down, add more water or stock.

When the meat is tender, remove it for carving, take out the lemon, onions, and celery, and make gravy in the pot. A quart is none too much if you plan to freeze some of the beef. That means you need a quart of drippings plus water to make up the amount. They can be thickened by adding ¼ cup cornstarch mixed with water to dissolve it (the proportions being 1 tablespoon cornstarch to thicken each cup of liquid).

Return sliced beef to the gravy to reheat or serve it in slices with the gravy separate.

Of course, those onions cooked with the meat are still good to eat. You might purée them and add them to the gravy. You could add potatoes, carrots, and other vegetables to the pot roast the last hour of cooking for the first dinner.

It is easier to slice the meat cold for the freezer. Package it in amounts to make a meal. Makes 2 dinners for 6 or 1 dinner for 12.

Chocolate Mousse

Nobody ever tells you, but by rights, a great mousse should sit for three or four days so the flavors can settle into that gorgeous consistency that's not a custard, not a whip, but what makes mousse mousse. However, who thinks that far ahead? We were meeting a 3:10 train when I realized we had no dessert planned for dinner that night. The following is what resulted. It needs four hours in the freezer or the ice cube section of your refrigerator. Frankly, it tastes even better one day later.

2 packages (6 ounces each)
    semi-sweet chocolate bits
½ cup water
1 stick butter
4 tablespoons instant coffee

10 tablespoons dark rum
    (more, if you like it) or
    brandy
1 pint heavy cream

Melt the chocolate with the water in a pan or double boiler over a low flame. Add butter, instant coffee and rum, and stir until you have a smooth sauce. Cool.

Whip the cream. Fold the cool sauce into the whipped cream. The mixture will be runny. Pour into a small soufflé dish, or individual pots, or paper cups or coffee cups. Chill in freezer, or ice cube compartment for at least 4 hours or overnight. Or, you can cook ahead and chill in refrigerator for 1–3 days. Serves 6–8.

THE NO-FRYING FRIED CHICKEN MENU

*Oven-Fried Chicken**
*Spinach Salad**
*Mock Monkey Bread**
*Pecan Pie** (*with or without Vanilla Ice Cream*)

When To Cook:

Oven-Fried Chicken: You can dip the chicken in the morning; get all ready to bake and refrigerate until cooking time. Or this will take about an hour and a half just before dinner.

Spinach Salad: You can prepare the spinach, crisp bacon, egg and salad dressing ahead of time. Assemble at dinner.

Mock Monkey Bread: Prepare the bread anytime the day of your dinner. Bake just before dinner.

Pecan Pie: Make in the morning, and let it warm in your already warm oven during dinner. (You could whip it together easily enough during the hour preceding dinner, but it would crowd your oven which this menu pretty much fills as is.)

Oven-Fried Chicken

A good quick way to get crisp chicken without standing over a frying pan.

This is a good time to say something about chicken. Either chickens are getting smaller; or our appetites are increasing; or we've been fooling ourselves. But the "normal" fryer-chicken you buy will *really* serve only 2–3 people. It would be better to allow 1 pound of chicken per serving in this and other chicken recipes.

4–6 pounds chicken, cut up
1 cup seasoned bread crumbs (or use cracker meal; crumbled packaged stuffing mix; crumbled potato chips mixed with garlic salt; crumbled barbecue chips; cornflake crumbs; rice cereal crumbs—whatever you have)

Dipping Mix
½ cup sour cream *or milk*
1 tablespoon lemon juice
1 teaspoon Worcestershire sauce
1 teaspoon celery salt
½ teaspoon paprika
2 cloves garlic, crushed
Salt and pepper

Wipe chicken with paper towels. Pour crumbs into a flat dish. Mix ingredients for the dipping mix. Dip each chicken piece, first into the mix, then into the crumbs. Arrange in a large greased shallow pan, skin side up and in one layer only, so the chicken will brown and crisp. Bake uncovered at 350° for 1 hour. Serves 4–6.

Variation: Mix 1 cup of crushed packaged herb-stuffing with ⅔ cup of grated Parmesan cheese. Season with garlic salt, chopped parsley and pepper.

Spinach Salad

1 pound fresh spinach
1 hardboiled egg, chopped
½ pound bacon

Dressing:

½ cup salad oil
⅛ cup wine vinegar
1 tablespoon white wine
1 teaspoon soy sauce
½ teaspoon sugar
½ teaspoon dry mustard
⅛ teaspoon curry powder
¼ teaspoon salt
¼ teaspoon garlic powder
½ teaspoon cracked black pepper

Wash, dry, and chill the spinach leaves. Tear into bite-size pieces. Fry the bacon until it's crisp. Crumble, combine with egg and sprinkle over spinach. Toss. Combine the ingredients for the dressing in a covered jar. Shake well, and chill. Add salad dressing to leaves and toss again. Serves 4–6.

Mock Monkey Bread

Real monkey bread is a fun raised-dough affair where everyone pulls away his portion. This recipe gives you the fun without the work.

2 packages prepared refrigerator buttermilk biscuits	½ cup melted butter or margarine

Remove biscuits from package; cut each in half. Dip each half in melted butter and place in a 9×5-inch loaf pan, or small casserole. Build up layers until all the biscuits are used up. Bake according to package directions, and turn out onto a serving board. Each person pulls out his portion. Serves 4–6.

Pecan Pie

3 beaten eggs	1 teaspoon vanilla
1 cup sugar	1 cup pecans
1 cup dark Karo syrup	1 unbaked pie shell
2 tablespoons melted butter	

Mix the eggs, sugar, syrup, butter, vanilla and pecans. Pour into 9-inch pie shell. Bake 15 minutes at 400°. Reduce heat to 325° and continue baking for 30 minutes more.

SUPPER SOUPS

One-Pot Maine Fish Chowder*
Quick and Savory Rolls*
Paper-Plate Pies*
Coffee

When to Cook:

One-Pot Maine Fish Chowder—takes 24–48 hours to ripen, and is the kind of Sunday supper dish you can put together on a Friday and not worry about for the rest of the weekend.

Quick and Savory Rolls—make at the last minute.

Paper-Plate Pies—Can be made ahead and frozen. Or made in the morning and chilled all day in the refrigerator.

One-Pot Maine Fish Chowder

This authentic Maine recipe is well worth the 24 to 48-hour waiting time.

2 medium onions	The same weight of potatoes
⅔ stick butter	3 cups milk
1½ or 2 pounds fish (haddock or flounder is best)	Salt and pepper to taste

Chop the onions. Cut the fish into squares. Slice the potatoes into medium slices. Build up a soup pot (preferably enamel) as follows:

  a. Spread the bottom with the chopped onions and pieces of the butter.
  b. Lay on the sliced potatoes.
  c. Add enough water to come to the middle of the potato layer.
  d. Lay on the fish.

Cover the pot. Cook 15 to 20 minutes, or until the potatoes are barely done. Cool. Ripen in the refrigerator 24–48 hours. When ready to serve, add the milk. Heat through, but don't boil. Season to taste. Serves 4 (or more, depending on how hungry you all are).

Quick and Savory Rolls

Slice an 8-ounce tube of crescent dinner rolls into ¼-inch

slices. Arrange them on an ungreased baking sheet. Brush with melted butter. Sprinkle with grated cheese or crumbled onion soup mix. Bake 8 to 10 minutes at 375°. Makes 24 rolls.

Paper-Plate Pies

You can make this well in advance, and freeze it, or chill in refrigerator for several hours.

1 cup Rice Krispies	1 tablespoon grated lemon
3 eggs	rind
½ cup sugar	3 tablespoons lemon juice
	1 cup heavy cream

Crush cereal and sprinkle half the crumbs over bottoms of six 4½-inch pie pans or paper plates of the same size. Separate egg yolks from whites and beat whites until fluffy. Add sugar gradually, continue beating until stiff and smooth. Now beat in yolks very thoroughly. Stir in lemon juice and rind. Beat cream until stiff and mix gently or fold into egg mixture. Pour into each plate, sprinkle tops with remaining crumbs and freeze, or chill. Remove from freezer or refrigerator 30 minutes before dessert time. Serves 6.

> *Zuppa Di Clama (Italian Clam Soup)**
> *Italian Bread, cut into chunks*
> *Mom's Blueberry Cheese Pie**
> *Espresso Coffee (page 70)*

When To Cook:

Zuppa Di Clama: Can be made within an hour of eating. You could make the tomato sauce part any time: freeze or refrigerate up to 3 days; reheat while clams are steaming.

Mom's Blueberry Cheese Pie: Make the day before, or in the morning. Refrigerate.

* Recipe follows

Zuppa di Clama
(Italian Clam Soup)

¼ pound butter (1 stick)
½ cup olive oil
4 cloves garlic, cut into
    pieces
3 or 4 large onions, sliced
    and minced
1 large can (17 ounces)
    Italian plum tomatoes

Oregano, salt, pepper and
    sugar to taste
Clams or mussels (about 40)
½ cup white wine
½ cup water

Heat butter and oil, add garlic, and onions, and brown them. Stir in the tomatoes, mashing them in the pan. Season to taste, using a lot of oregano. Simmer, covered, for 30 minutes. While sauce cooks, scrub the clams or mussels to remove the sand (see procedure on page 206). Pour the wine and water into a large pot. Add the clams or mussels and steam until the shells open. Save the liquid.

Stir ½ cup or more of the clam broth into the onion-tomato mixture, depending on how thick you like the broth. Lay the steamed clams in large individual bowls. Pour the Zuppa over. Eat, dunking bread slices into the Zuppa as you go. Serves 4.

Mom's Blueberry Cheese Pie

Graham cracker crust (if you don't buy one):

16 graham crackers crushed
¼ pound melted butter
    (1 stick)

¼ cup sugar

Crush the graham crackers between two layers of wax paper. (Use a liquor bottle if you don't have a rolling pin.) Combine with the sugar and melted butter and press into a 9-inch pie pan.

Cheese filling:

2 eggs
4 packages (3 ounces each)
   cream cheese
½ cup sugar

½ pint commercial sour
   cream
½ teaspoon vanilla
Dash cinnamon

Beat the eggs with an egg beater or whisk until they are light and foamy. Add the other ingredients, beating well until the mix is smooth. Pour this filling into the graham cracker crust. Bake 20 minutes at 375°. Cool.

Blueberry topping:

1 #2 can blueberries in
   heavy syrup
Lemon juice to taste (about
   2 tablespoons)

1 tablespoon butter
2 teaspoons cornstarch

Drain syrup from blueberries. Mix 3 tablespoons of syrup with cornstarch to form a smooth mix; heat remaining syrup over a low fire. Stir in cornstarch. Add lemon juice and butter. Cook for several minutes, stirring constantly, until syrup becomes thick. Remove from fire and add blueberries. Cool. When the cheese pie is also cool, spread the blueberries evenly over the top. Refrigerate and serve cold. You can make this a day ahead.

Fresh strawberry topping:

1 pint fresh strawberries

1 cup strawberry jelly

Wash, hull and dry the berries. Arrange them over the top of the cheese pie. Heat jelly in saucepan to melt it; when it is cool, but not cold, pour it over the berries.

THE HAMBURGER MENU

Hero Hamburgers* or Hamburger Pie*
Zucchini Crisps* (or Corn on the Cob)
Tossed Green Salad
Ice Cream Jumble*
Coffee

When To Cook:

Hero Hamburgers: You can panfry the hamburgers in the morning and let stand. You can also scoop out the bread then. But the final putting together should wait until just before dinner, or the loaf may get soggy.

Hamburger Pie: Make at the last minute.

Zucchini Crisps: Can be made early in the day. Warm on a cookie sheet in the oven at serving time. Or get the zucchini ready in the morning. Deep fry just before serving.

Ice Cream Jumble: Can be prepared anytime ahead, but needs a minimum of 6 hours.

Hero Hamburgers

Butter	1 loaf French bread
6 hamburger patties (about 1½ pounds lean ground beef)	Olive oil
	Lemon juice
	1 can flat anchovies, drained

Panfry the hamburgers quickly in butter but don't overdo them; they should be pink inside, lightly brown outside. Split the bread lengthwise. Scoop out the soft center. Spread the bottom half with olive oil. Sprinkle with lemon juice, and

* Recipe follows

line with anchovies. Top with hamburger patties. Cover with
the top half of loaf. Wrap in foil. Bake 15 minutes in a
300° oven. Slice at the table. Serves 4 for main dish or
buffet supper. Sliced thinner, will serve 8 as appetizer.

Hamburger Pie

This is a ten-minute deal in the oven that comes the closest
to tasting like "grilled chopped steak" we've ever had.

2 pounds round steak, ground once	Salt
	Butter

Salt the hamburger, handling it as little as possible. Pat it
into a 9″ greased pie plate, shaping the meat to fit the dish.
Top with gobs of butter. Broil as close to the heat as possible
for 5 minutes. Remove from oven. To turn over the meat,
slide it onto a dinner plate. Invert the pie plate over the
meat. Holding onto the dinner plate, turn the whole business
over. Top again with gobs of butter. Broil 5 minutes for
crusty on the outside, rare on the inside. Serve in wedges
with chopped chives and the pan juices sprinkled on top.
Serves 4.

To serve more, use another pie plate, not a larger pan. The
pie is equally good served with sautéed mushrooms or
Stroganoff Sauce (see Index).

Zucchini Crisps

4 zucchini	Garlic salt
Salt	Oil (or fat) for frying
Flour for dredging	Lemon wedges

Wash the zucchini and trim off the ends. Do not peel. Cut
into long strips about ¼″ thick; then into pieces about 3″
long. Sprinkle with salt; drain for 1 hour in a large strainer
or colander to eliminte excess juices.

Shake zucchini strips in a paper bag holding flour mixed
with a dash of garlic salt. Heat about an inch of oil in a large

skillet. When the oil is very hot, fry the zucchini until crisp and a very light brown. Drain on paper towelling. Serve with lemon wedges. Serves 4–5 as a side dish; 8–10 if you serve as a cocktail appetizer.

To cook ahead: After draining zucchini on paper towels, spread them out on a cookie sheet. Either keep warm in a low oven until serving, or reheat at serving time.

Ice-Cream Jumble

This is a quick, no-cook way to fancy up plain ice cream. You just have to remember to get it into the freezer or ice cube section of your refrigerator by noon of the day you want to have it—or the day before. It's also a fine way to use up dribs and drabs of cookies.

1 pint ice cream	¼ cup brandy
1 cup crumbled cookies	¼ cup shredded coconut

Set the ice cream in a large bowl to soften. Use any kind of cookies you have (mix them up; it doesn't matter and it's a good chance to get rid of the last of boughten cookies). Crumble them up with your fingers to make 1 cup. The crumbs should be large. With two forks, stir the crumbs thru the ice cream. Add the brandy and coconut. Turn into a small casserole, or use the ice cube tray from your refrigerator or parfait glasses. Freeze at least 6 hours. The texture will be softer than ice cream, but still firm. Spoon into glasses or bowls. Serves 4.

STEWS, RAGOUTS AND MISH-MASHES

Hunter's Stew*
Packaged refrigerator biscuits
Quick Apple-Mince Pie*
Coffee

When To Cook:

Hunter's Stew: A wonderful dish to cook ahead and carry to your vacation house. Or you can make it the day before. Or the same day.

Quick Apple-Mince Pie: This is a same-day quickie, using prepared pie crust and canned apples. Make and bake in the morning; or put together in the morning and bake during dinner to serve hot; or make and bake just before dinner.

Hunter's Stew

½ pound salt pork, cubed
½ pound salami, sliced and
    cut into ½ inch strips
1 large broiler-fryer chicken
    (3 to 4 pounds) cut up
4 whole carrots, pared
2 leeks or green onions,
    sliced 1 inch thick
4 sprigs parsley or 4
    tablespoons parsley
    chopped
2 whole cloves
1 bay leaf
¼ teaspoon crushed thyme

1 tablespoon salt
½ teaspoon pepper
3 beef bouillon cubes
3 cups hot water or 1 can
    (1 pound, 13 ounces)
    tomatoes
1 cup dry white wine
2 packages (10 ounces each)
    frozen California Brussels
    sprouts
¼ cup flour
¾ cup water

To cook ahead: Brown pork and salami in Dutch oven or large saucepan; remove and reserve. Brown chicken in the hot drippings; then drain off drippings. Return pork and salami. Stir in carrots, leeks, parsley, seasonings, bouillon cubes, hot water and wine. Cover and simmer 45 minutes, until chicken and vegetables are tender. Refrigerate up to 2 days or freeze. (If you are proceeding with the recipe, add the Brussels sprouts now and continue with recipe.)

30 minutes before eating: Reheat slowly on the stove, about 15 minutes. Add Brussels sprouts; cover and continue

½ cup flour
✓ for topping

cooking 10 to 15 minutes, until sprouts are just tender.
Blend together flour and the ¾ cup water; stir into stew.
Stir over medium heat until slightly thickened. Serves 6–8.

X **Quick Apple-Mince Pie**

Divided

1 ready-to-bake piecrust
2 cups mincemeat
3 cups canned sliced apples,
     drained

1 cup sugar – *less sugar*
1 tablespoon lemon juice
½ cup flour
¼ cup butter or margarine

Turn mincemeat into unbaked pie shell. Sprinkle ½ cup
sugar (depending on tartness of apples) and lemon juice
over the apples. Arrange over mincemeat. Mix together the
remaining ½ cup sugar and flour. Cut in butter until mixture is crumbly. Sprinkle mixture over apples. Bake at 450°
for 10 minutes. Reduce oven temperature to 325°. Bake 45
minutes longer. Yield: one 9-inch pie.

> *Cold Jambalaya**
> *Salt Sticks** or *Brown-and-Serve Rolls*
> *Bananas 'n Ginger**
> *Coffee*

This is a midsummer night's no-real-cooking delight. You
could even picnic with this dinner, bringing bakery rolls or
French bread.

When To Cook:

Cold Jambalaya: Make part of the salad the day before.
Assemble at the last minute. If you've had rice on your
menu earlier in the week, cook double and have the 2 cups
for this recipe all ready.

Salt Sticks: Prepare in the morning. Bake just before serving.

Bananas 'n Ginger: Put together just before serving time.
For a picnic, put a portion in a paper bowl. Cover with a
second bowl. Put a rubber band around.

* Recipe follows

Cold Jambalaya

1 pound frozen deveined
    shelled raw shrimps
2 cups rice, cooked
¼ cup bottled Russian salad
    dressing
¼ cup lemon juice
¼ cup mayonnaise or salad
    dressing
1 clove garlic, minced
¼ teaspoon leaf thyme,
    crumbled

¼ teaspoon bottled red
    pepper seasoning
1 can (1 lb.) ham
3 medium-size tomatoes
1 can or jar (4 ounces)
    pimentoes, drained and
    diced
1 head Bibb lettuce,
    separated into leaves

Cook shrimps, following label directions; drain. Place in medium size bowl. Place the cooked rice in a second bowl. Blend the Russian dressing and the lemon juice in a cup; drizzle 2 tablespoonfuls over the shrimps and 2 tablespoonfuls over the rice; toss each lightly; chill. Blend remaining dressing mixture with mayonnaise or salad dressing, garlic, thyme, and red pepper seasoning; chill. You can do this much the day before.

When ready to finish the salad, dice the ham and 2 of the tomatoes. Set aside 6 shrimps for garnish; fold remaining shrimps, ham, pimentos, diced tomatoes, and dressing into the rice mixture; spoon into a lettuce-lined deep serving dish. Cut the remaining tomato into 6 slices; place, overlapping, in a row over the rice mixture; top each with a shrimp and a tiny sprig of parsley, if you wish. Serves 6.

Salt Sticks

Cut unsliced bread into finger-length strips (about 1 inch thick—4 inches long). Brush on melted butter. Sprinkle well with coarse salt; brown 10–12 minutes in a hot oven (400°).

Bananas 'n Ginger

Cut bananas in half lengthwise (1 to a person). Cover with

chopped preserved ginger. Sprinkle with 1 tablespoon of the ginger syrup. Serve with whipped cream or ice cream.

Mediterranean Lamb Bake*
Green Salad with Watercress and Sliced Raw Mushrooms
Hot rolls
Paper Plate Pies (see Index)

When To Cook:

Mediterranean Lamb Bake—Put together in the morning; bake at night. Or, cook ahead; partially bake; reheat just before serving.

Green salad—Prepare salad greens and a dressing of your choice in the morning. Toss at dinner time.

Paper Plate Pies—Can be made ahead and frozen. Or made in the morning and chilled all day in the refrigerator.

Mediterranean Lamb Bake

What's nice about this is the rice cooks with the meat to make it a one-dish dinner.

1 eggplant	1 envelope instant beef broth
2 pounds lean lamb (boneless shoulder cut) cut in 1-inch cubes	1 tablespoon salt
	1 tablespoon basil
	½ teaspoon sugar
1 clove garlic, minced	½ teaspoon pepper
1 large onion, chopped	1 teaspoon rosemary
3 medium tomatoes, diced	1½ cups uncooked rice
2 cups water	Oil

To cook ahead: Pare and cut the eggplant in ½-inch cubes. Brown in oil. Drain. Brown the lamb and set aside. Sauté the chopped onion and minced garlic until soft. Stir in the tomatoes, water, beef broth, salt, basil, sugar, rosemary, and pepper. Bring to a boil. Then simmer for five minutes.

Make two layers each of eggplant, lamb and uncooked

rice in an eight-cup baking dish. Pour sauce over. Cover. Bake at 375° for one hour. Refrigerate up to 2 days.

30 minutes before eating: Heat, covered, in a 325° oven. Serves 6.

> *Edith's Lasagna**
> *Garlic Bread (see Index)*
> *Tossed Green Salad with Garlic French Dressing*
> *Summer Fruit Bowl (see Index)*
> *Coffee*

When To Cook:

Edith's Lasagna can be assembled the day before or the morning of dinner. Bake just before serving.

Summer Fruit Bowl needs to be put together early in the day to let the flavors blend. The syrup for the fruit can be prepared the day before.

Edith's Lasagna

Edith Hills Coogler, Woman's Editor of the Atlanta *Journal,* sent me such a delightful description of the lasagna recipe below, I am passing it on exactly as writ. You can put everything together the day before or that morning, and simply bake as described.

Edith's description

"I am sending you my most popular recipe. You heap the plates each time and even so, frail young girls want *thirds.* It is of my own devising after I studied about 50 other lasagna recipes and adapted them into a low-cal version, or at least *lower* cal and much more delicate. Since all lasagna recipes are time-consuming, this is no worse than the others. I can't tell you how many it serves since the nuts will go on eating it as long as you replenish the plates." [Figure 6 very large to 10 small portions.]

3 pounds ground chuck
30 (approximately) ounces
   Marinara sauce flavored
   with ½ tablespoon
   powdered oregano (or
   make your own sauce
   from tomato sauce and
   oregano until you can
   definitely taste the
   oregano)

½ teaspoon salt
10 to 12 ounces wide egg
   noodles
2 pounds small-curd cottage
   cheese or ricotta cheese
1 pound mozzarella cheese,
   sliced thin
8 ounces grated Parmesan
   cheese

To cook ahead: Brown meat in a heavy, large skillet without oil. Drain in a strainer. Return to pan, add sauce and seasonings, and simmer one to three hours.

Cook egg noodles according to package directions and add a little olive oil to keep them from sticking after you have drained them.

Fill two standard, teflon-lined loaf pans measuring approximately 9¼×5¼×2½ inches, making two layers, each as follows: Meat sauce, Noodles, Cottage cheese or ricotta, Mozzarella, and Parmesan. Top the second layer with more sauce and more Parmesan cheese.

30 minutes before eating: Bake in a 350° oven.

Two-Pot Paella*
Fruits in Liqueur (see Index)—Cookies (from bakery)
Coffee

When To Cook:

Two-Pot Paella—Let's face it, paella is a project. But for a special weekend, this method at least allows you to prepare most of it the day before, and put together at the last minute. I don't recommend freezing, because I've never been satisfied with the rice texture afterwards.

Fruits in Liqueur—make in the morning.

* Recipe follows

Two-Pot Paella

Paellas are as personal as toothpaste, it seems. And this is mine because I hate cooking rice *with* chicken as in other recipes. Uncooked traitors always seem to sneak under the chicken wings. Also the brown unpolished cooperative rice used in Spain is difficult to find here. I've found this method of cooking rice and chicken separately to be foolproof. The beer is a must according to a Cuban friend.

For the chicken pot:

2 frying chickens, cut up into 8 pieces each, seasoned with 1 teaspoon oregano, fresh ground black pepper, pinch of thyme, 1 clove garlic, crushed, 1½ teaspoons salt, 1 teaspoon vinegar
6 tablespoons olive oil
2 ounces cooked ham, cut in strips

1 chorizo (Spanish sausage) sliced (use Italian sweet sausage if you can't find chorizos)
1 ounce salt pork, chopped
1 onion, chopped
1 green pepper, chopped
½ teaspoon ground coriander
1 teaspoon capers

For the rice pot

2½ cups raw rice
2 cups beer
2 cups chicken broth
1 teaspoon saffron (or more, depending on taste)
3 tablespoons tomato sauce

1 pound raw shrimp, shelled and deveined
1½ pounds lobster meat, cooked
1 can peas
1 can chick-peas

For garnish

1 quart mussels
1 dozen small clams
1 jar pimentoes

Olives (optional)
Lemon quarters
3 tablespoons chopped parsley

To cook ahead: Brown the seasoned chicken in the olive oil. Add the rest of the "chicken pot" ingredients. Cover, and cook over a low fire for 20 minutes, or until the chicken is tender.

In the "rice pot" (use a casserole large enough to hold the works and also serve in): brown the rice in a little olive oil. Add the beer, chicken broth, saffron, and tomato sauce. Mix well and cook rapidly, covered, for 20 minutes. After 10 minutes, add the shrimp.

When the liquid is absorbed and the rice is done, stir in the lobster meat, peas, and chick-peas. Stir in the contents of the chicken pot. Cool and refrigerate.

About 1 hour before eating: Bring the paella pot to room temperature. Heat in a very slow oven (325°).

Clean the clams and mussels in several changes of cold water. About 15 minutes before serving, steam them on a rack or colander in a kettle. Pour 1 cup of water in the bottom (or beer, which is divine). Steam until they open.

To serve: Strain enough of the clam broth over the hot paella to make it moist, but not mushy. Garnish with the steamed clams, mussels, pimentoes and olives (sliced), and lemon quarters. Sprinkle chopped parsley over all. Serves 8–10.

Also see Index for Paella Fría.

Variation: For a Seafood Paella, you can eliminate the chicken pot and double the seafood ingredients.

> *Posole**
> *Tipsy Beans**
> *Tortillas (optional)*
> *Tossed Green Salad with Garlic French Dressing*
> *Flan (a custard mix to buy and prepare according to*
>   *package directions)*
> *Coffee*

This Way-Out-West menu is a variation of the popular Spanish and Mexican rice and beans . . . a hearty supper which you can cook ahead for a winter's night.

When To Cook:

Posole: Cook 2 or 3 days ahead. Turn into a casserole and

reheat in a slow oven at serving time. Or make, starting about 1½ hours before dinner.

Tipsy Beans: This is a lovely cook-and-travel-with dish. Cook 2 or 3 days ahead, or make in the morning.

Posole

Can be a hearty main dish, or an accompaniment, depending on how much pork you use.

2 pounds pork cutlet or tenderloin as a main dish; ½ pound as an accompaniment. Trim the fat and cut into small pieces.

Water; use 2 cups for 2 pounds pork; ⅔ cup for ½ pound pork

1 can (1 lb. 13 oz.) white or yellow hominy
1 small onion, chopped
2 cans green chili peppers, chopped finely
1 tablespoon chili powder

Simmer the pork in water, covered, until tender. Add all other ingredients. Cook over low heat, uncovered, until virtually all liquid is absorbed. Serves 4–6.

Tipsy Beans

2 cups pinto beans (1 pound package)
1 tablespoon salt
2 garlic cloves
¼ pound pork fat, cut into strips

1 tablespoon bacon fat
1 medium tomato
1 green pepper
1 onion
1 can beer

To cook ahead: In saucepan, cover beans with water seasoned with salt, add garlic cloves and pork fat, and cook until beans are tender, about 3 hours. Drain beans and reserve liquid. In an earthenware casserole, heat bacon fat and sauté the tomato, green pepper, and onion, all chopped until vegetables are soft. Stir in beans and let them simmer with other ingredients for about 5 minutes. Add reserved liquid and simmer beans for about 10 minutes. Add a can of your favorite beer to the pot. Stir thoroughly into beans. Cool and refrigerate.

45 minutes before eating: Heat in a 325° oven. Serve with posole and tortillas; or over rice. Serves 6–8.

> *Baked Spaghetti Mish-Mash**
> *Bread with Garlic or Other Butters**
> *Hot Brandied Fruit*—Macaroons (from the bakery)*
> *Coffee*

When To Cook:

Baked Spaghetti Mish-Mash—is a wonderful crowd dish. You can make it up to two days ahead and pop it in the oven an hour before dinner. This dish travels well, but is not good for freezing because the vegetables will get mushy.

Bread with Garlic or Other Butters—can be made ahead and frozen; or made in the morning and heated through at dinner time.

Hot Brandied Fruit—is the easiest crowd dessert ever. The sauce can be made in the morning. Canned fruits (mostly) get put together and heated at dinner time.

Baked Spaghetti Mish-Mash

Make it as is, or add sausages, more mushrooms and a little red wine.

2 pounds thin spaghetti,
    cooked and drained

Sauce:

½ pound bacon, diced
3 onions, sliced
3 pounds chopped raw beef
3 green peppers, chopped
3 tablespoons chopped
    parsley
1 can kidney beans

1 package (9–10 ounces)
    frozen peas
2 cans (1 pound 12 ounces
    each) Italian plum
    tomatoes
½ pound mushrooms, sliced
Salt, pepper, oregano to taste

Plus
½ pound (8 ounces)
  Parmesan cheese, grated

To cook ahead: Cook the spaghetti *al dente;* drain and reserve it. In a large, deep skillet, heat the bacon. Add onions and fry to a golden brown. Add the beef and brown quickly. Add the green peppers, parsley, beans, peas, tomatoes and mushrooms. Simmer 5 minutes, just to heat through. (The peas will be uncooked; they finish later, during the baking.) Season to taste.

In a large baking dish, alternate layers of cooked spaghetti and the meat mixture. Refrigerate.

2 hours before eating: Sprinkle with grated cheese. Bake at 325° covered; 15 minutes before serving, uncover. Serves 12–14.

Bread with Garlic or Other Butters

Hot French or Italian loaves, buttered and spicy, are a must with steaks, spaghetti dinners, main-dish salads—so many foods. You can buy garlic bread ready to heat, but I'm not wild about the hydrogenated taste. Try making several loaves next time you serve garlic bread, and freeze some for future use.

The Bread

Use long loaves, or individual club rolls or heroes. There seem to be two schools of buttering the long loaves: slice the loaf lengthwise, butter each half and replace. Or slice down the loaf, not quite cutting through, and butter the front and back of each slice.

In all cases I like to wrap the buttered bread in foil. Heat 15 to 20 minutes in a hot oven (400°) and unwrap the foil at the last to let the bread get crusty.

* Recipe follows

Garlic butter:

For 1 loaf of bread, combine 1 stick of softened butter with 3 or 4 cloves of garlic, crushed (which is easier), or cut into fine pieces (which is more Italian). Add a dash of olive oil. You can sprinkle grated Parmesan over the buttered slices, if you like, or use one of the following herb butters.

Herb butters:

Cream butter with a variety of herbs such as chopped parsley and tarragon, chopped chives and chopped green onions, and chopped dill.

Mustard butter:

Cream 1 stick of butter with ½ cup chopped onions and 2 tablespoons chopped parsley. Split bread the long way. First, spread on the herbed butter. On top of that, spread 2 tablespoons of prepared mustard. Sprinkle sesame seeds over all. Heat with each half open.

Hot Brandied Fruit

This is a good stomach-warming winter dessert for a crowd. If you're skiing for the day, put all the fruits, except the bananas, together. Get the sauce ready. Combine and heat at serving time. Buy *small* cans of all the fruits to serve 12; *large* cans to serve 20.

2 oranges, their juice and rind	1 can figs in syrup
1 pint brandied peaches	4 bananas
1 pint brandied grapes	½ cup raisins
1 can cooked prunes	¼ cup sugar
1 can pineapple chunks	¼ cup water
1 can bing cherries	Brandy to taste

Juice the oranges. Cut the rinds into strips and simmer in the sugar and water until the orange rinds are transparent. Add the orange juice and all the syrups from the canned fruit. Heat but don't boil. Add brandy to taste.

Just before serving (during dinner), mix all the fruits gently into the warm sauce. Simmer until hot. Serve. Serves 12–20 depending on the amount of fruit.

TO COOK AT THE TABLE

Stroganoffs

You can make stroganoff from practically any meat or seafood, it being no more than a flavorsome sour cream sauce with, usually, mushrooms and meat. The method of browning the meat, cooking the sauce separately, and then combining at the last minute allows you to cook ahead. Also, you can keep your beef rare and your seafood tender that way. (The long-cooking stroganoffs produce shoe-leathery meat!)

Here's some to choose from. Serve any of these with noodles or rice.

*Beef, Shrimp or Chicken Stroganoff**
Buttered Noodles
*Vegetables the French Way** (*green beans, carrots or peas*)
*Fruites Maison**
Coffee

When to Cook:

Stroganoff: This method lets you prepare the day before or the morning of your dinner, assemble and reheat at the last minute.

Vegetables the French Way: Start in the morning; finish at dinner.

Fruites Maison: A do-it-yourself dessert for which fruit is prepared at the last minute.

The Basic Method:

Step 1: Sauté the beef, chicken, or shrimp and set aside. See below.

Step 2: Make sauce. You can do this much ahead of time, combining the sauce and the meat after the sauce is cool. Refrigerate.

Step 3: At serving time, reheat stroganoff very slowly. Do not boil as the sour cream will curdle. When ready to serve, garnish with chopped parsley.

Beef Stroganoff

2 pounds beef tenderloin, sirloin, or filet cut in strips 2 inches long by ¼ inch thick and wide.

1 pound mushrooms, sliced
3 tablespoons butter

Sauté the mushrooms in the butter until golden. Set aside. Brown the meat quickly in the same pan, adding more butter if needed. Set aside. Use the pan to make the sauce.

Shrimp Stroganoff

2 pounds cooked shrimp, cut in narrow crescents
¼ teaspoon tarragon
1 pound mushrooms, sliced thin

Salt and pepper
6 tablespoons butter
Flour

Dust the shrimp lightly with a little flour mixed with tarragon, salt and pepper. Sauté the shrimp and mushrooms in the butter until golden. Set aside. Use the same pan to make the sauce, using chicken stock for your liquid, and leaving out the Worcestershire sauce.

Chicken Stroganoff

3 chicken breasts
Seasoned flour

1 pound mushrooms sliced thin
6 tablespoons butter

Bone and skin the chicken breasts and cut in half. Cut each half lengthwise into finger-length strips. Roll the strips in seasoned flour. Sauté in 4 tablespoons of the butter until tender and golden. Set aside. Sauté the mushrooms in the remaining butter. Set aside. Use the same pan for making the sauce, using chicken stock for your liquid, and leaving out the Worcestershire sauce.

Basic Stroganoff Sauce

4 tablespoons butter
4 tablespoons flour
½ teaspoon dried mustard
2 tablespoons tomato paste
¾ cup onion, finely chopped
2 tablespoons shallots or
    green onions, finely
    chopped

2 cups beef or chicken broth
    (depending on what
    meat you are using)
1 cup sour cream
Salt, pepper, Worcestershire
    sauce to taste
Chopped parsley to garnish

In the same pan in which you have browned your meat (see above), melt the butter. Sauté the onions and shallots until golden, but not brown. Stir in the flour, dried mustard, tomato paste and paprika, making a thick roux. Add in the beef or chicken broth a little at a time and cook, over a low flame, stirring until thickened.

At this point, taste for seasoning, adding salt, pepper, and Worcestershire sauce to your taste. Stir in the sour cream. When cool, add the meat. Refrigerate until needed. Complete as in Step 3 above. Makes sauce for 2 pounds of meat, which will serve 4–6.

Vegetables The French Way

Almost any vegetable except eggplant, zucchini, and artichokes can be cooked as follows to bring out the best flavor and texture.

Blanch or steam in a large pot until the vegetable is *almost,* but not quite, done. You really have to keep tasting, and the moment of truth comes sooner than you think. You can do this early in the day. Drain the vegetable and set aside.

Just before serving, reheat in lots of butter. Add salt and

pepper, chopped parsley, if you like. Experiment with other herbs: garlic, chopped onions, pinch of sugar (which some people feel brings out the sweetness), but not too much.

Fruites Maison

This do-it-yourself dessert works for either a buffet table, or for individual servings. What your guests do is spear fruits in season on individual picks. Dunk first into a bowl of chilled white wine, and then into confectioners' sugar. What you do is provide fruits, on large platters or individual plates, together with wine and sugar, as follows:

Whole strawberries
Fresh melon balls
Fresh pears, peeled, cored
    and quartered
Chilled white wine (Château
    d'Yquem, would be the

pièce de résistance, but
any dry or dessert wine
you like is fine. A
liqueur such as Cointreau
is also good)
Confectioners' sugar, sifted

For individual servings, put a filled wine glass in the center of the plate. Arrange the fruit around it. Serve the sifted sugar in small bowls at one side.

> *Sukiyaki**
> *Clever Hot Steamed Rice**
> *Bananas 'n Ginger* (*see Index*)
> *Tea*

When To Cook:

Sukiyaki is a cook-at-the-table dish. The preparation of the vegetables and meat takes some time, though, and can be done in the morning. The mushrooms must be soaked at least two hours ahead.

Clever Hot Steamed Rice can be started in the morning and finished just before serving time.

Bananas 'n Ginger can be put together just before serving

time. For a picnic, put a portion in a paper bowl. Cover with a second bowl. Put a rubber band around.

Sukiyaki

Sukiyaki can be cooked almost anywhere.

With plastic bags filled with the various ingredients, all sliced, and one of those new propane-fueled at-the-table cookers, you're free to sukiyaki it on the beach, in the woods . . . anywhere. Or plug an electric skillet in at an outdoor table. Even a skillet on a charcoal grill can be used. For plain kitchen cooking, take out the vegetables as they're done and keep them warm in the oven on an oven-proof platter.

2 pounds round steak, sliced thin (Ask your butcher to slice the steak on his machine, as thin as possible without tearing the meat. Or slice it yourself, after first freezing the steak slightly, which makes it easier)
1 package dried mushrooms
2 medium onions sliced

1 green pepper, sliced in thin strips
1 cup celery, sliced in 1½-inch strips
1 can bamboo shoots, sliced thin
1 bunch green onions, cut in 1-inch lengths, including the tops
1 package fresh spinach, washed and drained
2 tablespoons salad oil

Broth:
¼ cup sugar
¾ cup soy sauce

Liquid from the mushrooms
½ cup sake or sherry

Soak the mushrooms in water to cover at least two hours. Remove the mushrooms and slice thin. Save the mushroom liquid. Combine the sugar, soy sauce, sake, and ¼ cup of the mushroom liquid into a broth. Assemble the other ingredients on a tray or platters. Now you're ready to cook.

Heat oil to smoking in a skillet. Add the sliced onions, green pepper, and celery. Stir fry for one minute. Pour over the broth. Cook a few minutes. Add bamboo shoots, mushrooms, and spinach. Cook 3 to 5 minutes. Push the vegetables to one side and add the meat and green onions. Cook 1 or 2 minutes or until the meat is done the way you like it.

To serve: According to Ralph and Helen Dreyfuss who brought the recipe back from Tokyo with them, the proper Japanese way to serve, if you're cooking at the table, is to dish up each group of vegetables and meat as soon as it's cooked. Or, if your wok or pot or skillet is large enough, wait and serve everyone at once when the meat is done. Serve with hot steamed rice. Serves 6–8.

Clever Hot Steamed Rice

"Clever," because in this method you don't have to be worrying about what the rice is doing (probably getting gummy in the old methods) while you're focused on the sukiyaki or whatever else you want to serve this with.

Anytime on serving day: Allowing 1 cup of rice for 4 servings, simply drop it (much like spaghetti) into a large amount of boiling, salted water. Stir occasionally. When the rice is *al dente*, about 20 minutes, drain and wash with cool water. In this method, there is no need to wash the rice first. All the grains stay separate. At this point, the rice sits until just before dinner. (Or can be used as is in dishes calling for cooked rice.)

25 minutes before serving: Pile the rice into a large strainer or colander. Set the strainer into a pan of boiling water. Cover. Heat over low flame until the rice is well heated through. If you don't have a cover that will fit over your strainer, use foil. For a picnic: Steam the rice as above. Pile it hot into an icebucket or wide-mouthed thermos; or put a small casserole into an insulated bag.

Variation: For more of a flavor to serve with other dishes, heat the rice in a frying pan with a fair amount of butter. Season with salt, pepper, chopped parsley.

Add any one of these, if you like: pine nuts; raisins; cooked peas or black beans; finely diced green pepper.

Fondues

Everybody cooks his own piece of food on a long fork dunked into hot oil or cheese (or chocolate, page 171, or whatever the fondue base is). Then into a variety of sauces.

It's nice to have an electric fondue pot, which comes with its own stand, but any pot-shaped chafing dish will do for most fondues; and a wider ceramic dish with warming stand is good for cheese and chocolate fondue. There is no reason why you can't just bring a pan of oil to the table and keep it hot on an electric or alcohol burner.

I think it's too hard to try and feed more than 4–6 people over one fondue pot, unless your fondue is part of an appetizer buffet. So for more people, use more pots.

A Fondue Dinner*: Cheese, Beef, Shrimp or Sausage or
    a combination
Tossed Green Salad
Warmed French Bread
Bowl of Fruit
Coffee

This is a perfect vacation dinner—one I call "group therapy" . . . very American brotherhoody, as well as an opportunity for instant analysis of your neighbors. Just watch who grabs whose fondue fork to spot deep-seated personality traits that might never show themselves so clearly again.

When to Cook:

Fondue: It takes just a few minutes ahead of time to prepare the foods (except for shrimp) and materials. Make the sauces, or get them ready, in the morning. Cook at the table.

Cheese Fondue

The new packaged cheese fondues are so good, it scarcely

seems worth starting from scratch any more. Doctor the basic mix like this:

Rub a clove of garlic around your fondue dish. Heat the cheese fondue according to package instructions. Add a jigger each of kirsch and white wine. Season to taste with nutmeg and a little more garlic. Serve with a basket of French bread in chunks. Spear a bread chunk on a long-handled fork; dip and twirl it through the cheese mixture until it's coated. Eat.

Picnic Fondue

These ingredients can be carried to wherever you're going. Just heat together in a medium saucepan over a grill or a fire, or sterno, or at home on the stove.

1 cup shredded cheddar cheese   ¾ cup beer
1 envelope cheese-sauce mix

Mix everything together, stirring. Use sesame breadsticks to dip with, or chunks of French bread stuck onto wooden sticks. Makes 1¼ cups of Fondue.

La Fondue Bourguignonne

4 cups cubed (1 inch cubes)   A small piece of raw potato
   tender beef such as   (to keep the oil from
   sirloin, filet mignon, etc.   spattering)
Vegetable oil   Sauces: below
Olive oil, optional

Fill your fondue pot half full with mostly vegetable oil, adding some olive oil for flavor. Heat the pot on the stove until the oil is bubbling. Then keep the oil bubbling at the table over an adjustable burner. Add the raw potato. At each guest's place, set a dinner plate, with a portion of raw meat cubes in the middle. If by any chance you've got divided plates, put individual portions of the sauces around the meat; otherwise, set out the sauces in small bowls. Flank the plates with a fondue fork, a dinner fork, and a spoon. Each guest spoons a sampling of the sauces around the rim of his own plate, cooks his own meat in the oil with the fondue fork, switches to the dinner fork, dips cooked meat in one or more sauces, and (at last) eats. [While he's eating, a fresh piece of meat can be cooking on the fondue fork.] Serves 4 or 5.

Shrimp Fondue

Prepare raw shrimps by shelling and deveining them. Rinse in cold water. Pat dry on paper towels. Cook in oil, as described above. Two pounds of shrimp will serve 4. Serve with cold dill sauce, hot curry sauce, or tartar sauce.

Sausage Fondue

Chunks of Italian sweet and hot sausages, German sausages, even hot dogs, can be cooked for a fondue. Try threading them on a fork with a cube of hard cheese, like a Swiss cheese. Don't let the cheese cook too long or it will melt into the oil. Serve with hot chili sauce.

Sauces for fondues:

Two or three sauces, hot and cold, give variety to a fondue dinner. Choose from these.

1. Bearnaise sauce: You can buy it in jars or mix, serve hot or cold.
2. Hollandaise sauce: also to buy.
3. Escoffier Sauce Diable: Buy it. Good just the way it is, cold.
4. Dill sauce: Mix 2 cups mayonnaise with ¼ cup lemon juice, 1 crushed garlic clove, 1 teaspoon dill, and salt to taste. Good as a dip for fish or for small cooked potato balls.
5. Hot chili sauce: Melt ½ cup butter. Add ½ cup chili sauce and ½ cup ketchup. Season with a dash of Tabasco sauce, a pinch of brown sugar. Heat.

6. Raw onion sauce: Mix ¾ cup minced onions with 1 tablespoon horseradish and 1 tablespoon sour cream.
7. Hot curry sauce: Melt ¼ cup butter in a saucepan. Stir in 2 tablespoons flour and 1 teaspoon curry powder (or to taste). Add 1 cup consommé. Cook over low heat, stirring, about 15 minutes. Strain. You can also serve this cold.

NO-MENU END-OF-THE-WEEKEND LEFTOVER RECIPES

Swedish Beef Salad*
No-Worry Curries made with In a Hurry Curry Sauce*
Cold Curry Salad Gauguin*
Fish Hash*
Whatever's-In-The-Icebox Fried Rice*
Sweet and Sour Vegetables*

Swedish Beef Salad

This would be nice to include in a smorgasbord.

2 cups cooked beef, cut in
    ½-inch dice
1 onion, minced
1 dill pickle, minced
1 apple, peeled and diced
2 stalks celery, diced

1 tablespoon pickled beets,
    minced
2 teaspoons liquid from the
    beets
½ cup mayonnaise (or
    enough to moisten)

Mix all the ingredients several hours before serving. Chill. Serves 4 as a main-dish salad.

No-Worry Curries

Almost any cooked meat or fish can be curried quickly and easily. Serve with boiled rice (which you'll make more of for another time), grated coconut, chopped peanuts, chopped parsley, and/or raisins for sprinkling on top. The sauce below is for 2 to 3 cups of diced cooked meat which will serve 3 or 4.

When To Cook?

a. Last minute, or
b. Make in the morning; reheat over low heat at serving time, or
c. Cook ahead up to 3 days before; or
d. Cook and freeze.

IN A HURRY CURRY SAUCE

2 onions, chopped
1 apple, chopped (optional)
½ cup chopped celery (optional)
½ cup butter
½ cup flour
1 to 2 tablespoons curry powder

¼ teaspoon salt
2½ cups hot liquid (consommé, chicken stock, milk, leftover gravy, meat juices— whatever you have)
2 teaspoons mint leaves

Sauté the onions (apple and celery) in butter until they are soft. Stir in flour, curry powder, and salt to make a thick paste. Let it brown. Slowly add the liquid, stirring over low heat until the sauce is thick. Add mint, if desired. Taste for seasoning. Add meat of your choice and heat through over a low flame.

Cold Curry Salad Gauguin

This is one of those rare delights because it works on so many levels. It's a one-dish meal. It uses a variety of ingredients you might be worrying about at the end of a weekend. And it's elegant enough for a party buffet. All cool and yellow, sprinkled with the green of chopped parsley, like a Gauguin painting.

When To Cook?

a. Last minute, or
b. Mix the meat, vegetables and rice the day before, or in the morning. Combine with cold curry sauce up to 3 hours before serving.
c. Cold Curry Sauce can be made up to a week ahead.

4 to 5 cups cold cooked rice
2 to 3 cups diced meat or seafood (You can use turkey, chicken, lamb, pork, beef, shrimp, lobster, or a jambalaya-type mixture)

2 to 3 cups chopped fresh vegetables (celery, cucumber, green pepper)
1 cup chopped parsley

Plus:

1 recipe Cold Curry Sauce (below)
3 tablespoons salad oil
1 tablespoon red wine vinegar

2 tablespoons chopped chives
Optional:
Pineapple chunks, water chestnuts, diced cooked bacon, diced hard-cooked eggs

Using two forks throughout to stir with, drizzle the salad oil and vinegar over the cold cooked rice. Stir to coat the grains. Stir in the meat and vegetables. Let stand at room temperature. Stir in the Cold Curry Sauce with ½ cup of the chopped parsley. Chill until serving time. Sprinkle the remaining parsley over. Serves 6–8.

COLD CURRY SAUCE

1 apple peeled, cored and sliced
2 onions, chopped
¼ cup butter
1 to 2 tablespoons curry powder
1 teaspoon crushed coriander seed (optional—if you don't have any, use just the curry powder)

1 teaspoon flour
About ¾ cup milk or coconut milk
2 teaspoons chopped fresh mint or 1 teaspoon dried (optional)
2 cups mayonnaise
Lemon juice to taste

Melt the butter. Sauté the apple and onions until they are soft. Add curry powder (according to your taste), coriander seed and flour. Add just enough milk or coconut milk to make a thick paste. Add the mint leaves. Cool. Stir the curry paste into the mayonnaise. Add lemon juice, salt and pepper to taste.

Fish Hash

Cold cooked fish (flake and measure in measuring cup)

An equal part of cold boiled potatoes (cut in small chunks and measure)

1 onion, grated

Butter or margarine for cooking

1 egg beaten

Ahead of Time: Flake the cold fish. Cut the potatoes in small chunks. Mix together with the grated onion. Add the egg. Taste for seasoning. Refrigerate or freeze.

30 minutes before eating: Melt butter in a large frying pan. When the butter is hot, press the hash in, and cook quickly to brown. Turn and brown on the other side. (If you want a delicious crusty hash, brown the second side under the broiler. Wrap the pan handle in foil, if it's made of wood.)

Whatever's-In-The-Icebox Fried Rice

As you can see by the ingredients, this is a good last-minute way to use up whatever's around. (You can prepare the diced vegetables and meat in the morning.)

1 cup any fresh uncooked vegetable; or combination, such as diced lettuce, tomatoes, celery, onions, green beans, cucumber, etc.

And/or 1 cup diced cooked meat, seafood, or crumbled bacon

And/or 1 cup any canned Chinese vegetable, such as bean sprouts, bamboo shoots, etc.

4 cups cooked rice

1 to 2 eggs, beaten

Cooking oil

2 to 3 tablespoons soy sauce

½ teaspoon salt

1 teaspoon sugar

Sauté the fresh vegetables first, quickly, in 2 tablespoons hot oil, just to soften. Add any canned vegetables (drained and rinsed through with cold water). Heat through. Remove all vegetables from the pan. Heat more oil. Break up the cold rice with a fork, or your hands, and fry quickly, stirring until well heated. Stir in the meat and the cooked vegetables. Add the seasonings, using soy sauce to your taste. Scramble in the beaten eggs by making a well in the center of the rice. When the eggs begin to set, scramble them through the rice. Serves 4–5.

Sweet and Sour Vegetables

This is a nice way to use bits of vegetables. The ones listed here are suggestions. Anything you like can be prepared this way.

Sauce:

4 tablespoons cornstarch or potato starch	1 cup sugar
1⅓ cups water	⅔ cup vinegar
6 tablespoons soy sauce	3 tablespoons ketchup
	Salt and pepper

Vegetables:

Onions, sliced	Bamboo shoots (canned. Drain and rinse in cold water)
Green peppers, sliced	
Mushrooms, halved	
Snowpeas (fresh or frozen)	3 tablespoons cooking oil

Make the sauce by blending cornstarch with some of the water; add in the other ingredients.

Heat the oil until it smokes, and sauté the vegetables. Salt and pepper them as you stir. Add the sauce. Cook for 2–3 minutes. Serve hot. Serves 6–8, depending on how many vegetables you use.

7

SOME PARTY PLOTS
Big, Small, Cheap, Expensive, Quick and Not-so Plots for Parties and Holidays and a way to give three Do's on the same weekend

"If the cocktails had been as cool as the soup,
If the soup had been as warm as the wines,
If the wines had been as old as the chicken,
If the chicken had been as plump as the maid,
If the maid had been as available as the hostess,
By Jove! It would have been a marvelous party!"

Anonymous French Diplomat

Styles

By Jove! What more marvelous place for a party than your vacation house. In your "pure playground for $250.00 down" you've got the space and the ambience to have the fun the ads promised you. Leave city party habits in the city.

In the first place, your pure playground may be miles and miles away from ice—if you run out of it. Or Schweppes—if you forgot to buy enough. So super list-making and thorough marketing are a must. Forget about sending Junior down the block for more napkins. And plan on cooking more than you'd ordinarily calculate. Invited guests have a way of turning up with house guests of their own.

On the other hand, your party styles can be much easier and simpler than back home. Unless you're set up, like one family I know, to "send the station wagon with the servants, children, and supplies up to the country early," forget about formal entertaining. Even the drop-dead dinner parties that follow can be served simply.

But "simply" doesn't mean without style. The style with which you do a party can make even hamburgers and beer a memorable occasion (as on a winter's night fireplace cook-in; guests in slacks; everyone cooking his own hamburger).

The way you serve and where you serve is what will give your party its special style.

(See "About Serving and Eating Styles," page 17.)

Plots For Holidays

The long holiday weekends (drive carefully, please) are, for us, either a foggy swirl of party-going and giving; or quiet, starve-all-day-because-Mom's-cooking-a-great-dinner dinners.

The menu ideas which follow give you your choice.

New Year's

(Either New Year's Eve or New Year's Day)

Give a "Nibblers and Gobblers" Buffet party, dinner or lunch (see Index), adding champagne or Danish Egg Nog (also listed in Index).

Or, if you don't want to do much cooking, this would be a fine time for the "Big Expensive No-Cook Wine Tasting" party which lets you have an open-house for any number of people.

Easter

The first "Same Food, New Faces" menu on page 179 is a wonderful ham dinner for the family and a few guests.

Since Easter weather, no matter where you are, is usually too warm for a large indoor crowd, and too cool for an outdoor party, why not handle a group of people with a "Make Your Own Omelettes" brunch (page 56). This could even be extended into an all-afternoon open-house. The omelettes are there to be made any time you want to.

Fourth of July and Labor Day

The two summer holidays are meant to be enjoyed outside, and there are several menus (see Index for page numbers) you'll have fun with interchangeably.

"Red, White, and Marvelous" lunch is perfect for a crowd in the afternoon. And I see nothing wrong with making a dinner out of it, either.

"Good Old American Barbecue" can be done for about a dozen people.

The "Real Nice Clambakes" are for half a dozen friends you're comfortable enough to be messy with. And if you want to go whole hog, do a beach clambake for as many people as you like.

Labor Day, especially, might be a good day for the "Big Cheap No-Cook Revenge Party." After all, you're not supposed to labor either.

Thanksgiving and Christmas

These are holidays where tradition is hard to beat. So I stuck with tradition in the "Old Fashioned Holiday Dinner" menu on page 163 to let you do a fair amount of cooking ahead. But there's a new twist to the turkey or chicken.

However, Thanksgiving or Christmas dinner in your second-house could just as well reflect the casual spirit I hope you're promoting there. If you're feeling casual try the "Winter Cook-In" dinner.

SMALL EXPENSIVE DROP-DEAD* DINNER PARTIES

Sometimes you want to make a party like James Beard is coming to dinner. Or the Pope. Anyway, you don't mind spending money, if not time, delighting perhaps a dozen people.

But you're still cooking in a second house where the graters, grinders, mortars and puree-ers may be non-existent.

These menus can be handled without special equipment, and while simple, they are considered classic.

There would be nothing wrong if you served the first course of these menus in the living room. Unless you've got help. Or, if you served buffet style. Just pay attention to the ambience—the look and arrangement of the dishes. Style adds to the drop-deadness. One hostess I know writes her menu on a large blackboard. Another serves dinner at the kitchen table with red-checked tablecloth and wooden plates. Or simply decorate your buffet table with wild flowers. The point is not to be formal—you can't really in a second house—but to create an atmosphere.

* Drop Dead means from delight

A Drop-Dead Summer Dinner For Six

You can cook as much of this dinner as you like the day before, which means you don't have to drop dead from fatigue preparing it.

Your second house is probably close to farms or farm stands offering all kinds of seasonal delights, well worth a short drive away from packaged supermarket tomatoes. So choose your vegetables for the Vegetables Vinaigrette from the freshest around. There is simply no substitute for fresh-pickedness.

> *Jellied Wine Consommé**
> *Cold Poached Salmon with Cucumber Sauce**
> *Cold Vegetables, Vinaigrette**
> *Cheese and warm sliced French bread*
> *Lemon Ices with Crème de Menthe**
> *Coffee*
> *Wine: The best dry white wine you can afford*

Jellied Wine Consommé

Start with 2 cans (13 ounces each) of a good brand of jellied consommé. Empty into a bowl undiluted. Add ¼ cup wine (or more to taste); use Madeira, Port, white wine, sherry. To be very elegant, stir in 1 or 2 tablespoons black caviar. Chill until set according to label instructions. Spoon into bowls. Garnish with chopped parsley on top and serve with lemon wedges. Serves 6.

Note: To jell a consommé from scratch, heat plain consommé. Add 1 envelope plain gelatin for each quart of soup.

Cold Poached Salmon

This is a lovely, summery, cook-ahead dish which you can cook the day before. You don't need a special pan. The foil method of oven poaching requires only the bottom of your oven broiler pan.

1 whole cleaned salmon, 5–8 pounds, split	Salt and pepper
1 teaspoon thyme	1 bay leaf
1 onion, thinly sliced	¾ cup dry white wine

Rinse the fish inside and out. Dry with paper towels. Place it lengthwise on a long double-fold sheet of quilted foil. Sprinkle the salmon inside and out with the thyme, onion, salt and pepper. Lay the bay leaf inside. Bring up the edges of the foil and move the whole business into the bottom of your oven broiler pan. (Cut off the head, if the fish won't fit). Pour the wine over. Seal foil completely around fish.

Bake in a 375° oven, 12–15 minutes per pound. The salmon is done when it flakes easily with a fork. Serves 6–12.

Open the foil and let the fish cool on it. Then refrigerate. Serve with one of the following mayonnaise dressings.

Cucumber Mayonnaise: Add a finely diced peeled cucumber to 2 cups mayonnaise. Squeeze in lemon juice to taste.

Horseradish Mayonnaise: Mix equal parts of mayonnaise and whipped cream. Add prepared white horseradish (1 to 2 tablespoons per cup) and salt to taste.

Vegetables Vinaigrette

Asparagus: (2 pounds fresh, if available; if not, 2 packages frozen). Steam, covered tightly, in as little salted water as possible, and until just tender not limp. Drain.

Green beans (or Zucchini): 2 pounds fresh if possible; if not, 2 packages frozen green beans cut French-style. Cook until barely tender in a minimum of salted water.

Mushrooms: Buy 1 pound mushrooms, white, with stems firmly in caps, as near equal in size as possible. Drop them into a lemon juice and water bath before marinating. Drain. Marinate raw, sliced vertically.

Tomatoes: Skin tomatoes by dunking them into boiling water for ten seconds. Slice crosswise. You will need 1 tomato per serving.

Use one or more of the vegetables listed (the amounts listed each serve 6 so reduce quantities as necessary), but marinate in separate bowls and serve in individual mounds, so flavors are distinct. The vegetables can be marinated in the vinaigrette dressing the day before the party.

Vinaigrette dressing

1 cup oil, a combination of olive oil and salad oil is excellent
⅓ cup wine vinegar
1 teaspoon salt
½ teaspoon dry mustard
Freshly ground pepper

½ cup chopped parsley
1 tablespoon chopped chives
1 tablespoon capers, drained and chopped
1 teaspoon sour pickle, chopped
½ teaspoon onion juice

Combine ingredients; stir well or shake in jar before using over vegetables.

Lemon Ices with Crème de Menthe

4 cups cold water
2 cups sugar
½ cup lemon juice

1 tablespoon finely grated lemon rind
Crème de menthe

Boil water and sugar together in saucepan until sugar dissolves; stir constantly (takes about 5 minutes). Cool slightly and add lemon juice and rind. Pour into refrigerator trays and set in freezer until firm. Serve in dessert coupes; pour 1½ tablespoon crème de menthe over each serving. Serves 6.

A Drop-Dead-Anytime Dinner (For Twelve)

This isn't as complicated as it looks. Buy the clams and have them opened the day of the dinner. Refrigerate. Make the potatoes; green beans; sauces for the steak; and sugar the berries in the morning. The steak has to be done at the last minute, but you can cocktail with your guests while it bakes, reheating the vegetables just before dinner is ready.

Clams on the Half Shell—Cocktail Sauce—Lemon Wedges
   (Allow 6 clams per serving)
Baked Steak with Mushrooms*
Potatoes Chantilly*—Sautéed Green Beans
Boston Lettuce Salad with Lemon French Dressing (see Index)
   (Buy 5–6 heads for salad for 12)
Brie Cheese—Hot Sliced French Bread
Strawberries with Raspberry Sauce*
Wine: A red Burgundy or Bordeaux

Baked Steak with Mushrooms

2 or 3 porterhouse steaks to weigh 10 pounds (you can have the tail ground and put back with a skewer)

Basting sauce
¼ cup Worcestershire sauce
1½ tablespoons salt
¼ teaspoon ground pepper
6 tablespoons softened butter
1 clove garlic, crushed
2 tablespoons minced onions

Mushroom sauce
1 pound mushrooms, sliced thin
3 tablespoons butter
½ teaspoon meat extract
   (or Worcestershire sauce; soy sauce; Sauce Robert; Escoffier sauce)
Salt, pepper
1 tablespoon chopped chives
1 tablespoon butter at end

Ahead of time: Mix together the ingredients for the *basting* sauce. Begin the *mushroom sauce* by sautéeing the mushrooms in butter until they are soft. Stir in the meat extract. Season to taste with salt and pepper. Add chives. Let stand until later.

About 30 minutes before dinner: Preheat your oven to 550°. Arrange the steaks in a shallow baking pan. Spread with half the basting sauce and bake for 12 minutes. Turn the steaks. Brush with the rest of the sauce and bake until done the way you like them. (About 15 minutes more, but you're safer inserting a meat thermometer after turning the steaks.) Keep the steaks warm on a serving platter while you finish the sauce.

Put the steak baking pan on top of stove. Heat and stir with ¼ cup water and 1 tablespoon butter. Bring to quick boil. Add the mushroom sauce to the pan juices. Heat through over low flame. Taste for seasoning. Pour over steaks and serve. Serves 12.

Potatoes Chantilly

Put 8 cups prepared instant mashed potatoes into a buttered casserole. Top with 1 cup heavy cream, whipped. Sprinkle with 1 cup grated Gruyère or Cheddar cheese. Heat at 375° until cheese is melted and bubbly.

Note: If you're cooking this menu with one oven, pop the potatoes into the oven about 5 minutes before steaks are done. When you take out the steaks, turn oven down. While you're finishing the sauce, the potatoes will finish.

Strawberries with Raspberry Sauce

A lovely quick dessert which you can make with either frozen raspberries or strawberries and use on "doctored" fruit (page 90) or ice cream.

2 quarts fresh berries (strawberries, raspberries, boysenberries, sugared and soaked in Cointreau or kirsch for at least 2 hours)

Sauce: 3 packages (10-oz. each) frozen raspberries

Thaw the frozen berries slightly. Whirl on high in blender for half a minute. Strain. "Doctor" with liqueur or not, as you prefer. Serve with sugared berries. Serves 12.

Without a blender: It's harder, but you can let the berries defrost and force through a strainer.

GOOD OLD AMERICAN BARBECUE FOR TWELVE

The pork, boned and flattened, slices down like steak. The beans are cooked ahead and reheated outside (if you have space). We found this menu perfect for hearty eaters (like home-from-fishing-or-sailing appetites). Consider a winter barbecue, too. Cook the meat outside, everything else in. Or use your fireplace.

> *Barbecued Loin of Pork—with Barbecue Sauce**
> *Rum Black Bean Casserole with Sour Cream**
> *Tossed Green Salad with Fruit* (*see Index*)
> *Lemon French Dressing* (*see Index*)
> *Fresh Berry Pie—Whipped Cream**
> *Coffee*

Barbecued Loin of Pork

This is a marvelous solution for a crowd of meat-lovers. And cheaper than steak. Our favorite beach butcher, Ed Mueller in Bridgehampton, was doubtful at first, but he agreed to bone the loin, close to the bone. We then had about an 18 inch long piece of solid meat which Ed flattened with a cleaver in the thicker spots. Then he split the bones into pieces—about three bones to a piece—which gave us in all, sliceable meat and spare-ribby bones for a dozen people. Ten pounds of pork loin, Ed said, would cost us eleven something for the meat and twenty-five dollars for the advice? which I am now passing on for free.

10 pound pork loin, boned
    and flattened

Marinate the pork loin and bones in the barbecue sauce

(below) all day at room temperature, or overnight in the refrigerator. Use your oven broiler pan, and cut the meat in half, if one piece is too long to fit into the pan.

Cook over a charcoal fire for 40–50 minutes, as follows. Brown the roast quickly on both sides, then cook, turning frequently until the meat feels hard to the touch. Pork must be well cooked. Baste from time to time with some of the barbecue sauce. About 20 minutes after starting the roast, add the bones to the grill. Then everything will come out at the same time. 10 minutes before serving, heat the pot of reserved barbecue sauce.

To serve: Slice the pork loin into thin slices (like slicing down steak). Arrange on a platter with the bones at one end . . . Serve with extra barbecue sauce on the side.

Barbecue Sauce For Pork Loin

2 onions, minced
½ cup finely diced celery
2 bottles (18 ounces each) prepared barbecue sauce (I like Open Hearth or Ann Page)

1 tablespoon dried mustard
1 teaspoon cumin seed
2 tablespoons chili powder
3 tablespoons lemon juice
10 drops Tabasco sauce

Sauté the onions and celery in bacon fat, or any oil, until they are golden. Use a large saucepan. Add all the other ingredients. Bring to a boil for two minutes. Use this as marinade for the pork loin (also good for chicken). While the meat is cooking, use some of the marinade for basting, but save most of it to heat for a sauce. Serves 12.

Rum Black Bean Casserole with Sour Cream

Spanish or Mexican with a bit of the Black Sea added, this casserole is one of our standbys for serving a crowd. It's good as is with barbecued spareribs, or any kind of roast meat. If you add a variety of sausages—chorizo, pepperoni,

Italian sweet sausage—you've got a main dish meal. You can make the casserole even two days before eating, as the flavor ripens on standing.

1½ pounds black beans	2 stalks celery with the
1 onion, sliced	leaves
3 strips bacon, cut into small	2 tablespoons flour
squares	2 tablespoons butter
1 tablespoon salt	½ cup dark rum
Pepper	6 dashes of Tabasco sauce
6 sprigs parsley	1 pint (2 cups) sour cream
1 bay leaf	

To cook ahead: Soak the beans overnight in water to cover. The next morning, most of the liquid will have been absorbed. Add five cups more of cold water to the pot; the sliced onions; salt and pepper; parsley; bay leaves; bacon; and celery. Bring to a boil, cover, and simmer the beans until tender. This will take about 1½ hours. Check the liquid as the beans cook, adding boiling water if too much cooks away.

Drain the beans, saving 2 cups of the liquid they were cooked in. Arrange the beans in a large (6 to 8 quart) casserole dish.

In a saucepan, melt the butter. Add flour to make a roux. Gradually add the bean liquid, rum and Tabasco. Cook stirring until the sauce thickens slightly. (At this point, you'd better taste for seasoning, particularly for salt and Tabasco sauce.) Pour the sauce over the beans and refrigerate, covered.

40 minutes before eating: When ready to serve, heat the bean casserole in a 350° oven, covered, for 15 minutes. Uncover, and continue heating another 15–20 minutes. Serve from the casserole, with a generous spoonful of sour cream on top of each serving. Serves 12.

Note: Anything left over, mixed with cooked rice and reheated gives you another dish for another meal.

* Recipe follows

Fresh Berry Pie

For each pie: (makes 2 pies to serve 12)

1 quart ripe strawberries, raspberries, or blueberries	2½ tablespoons corn starch mixed with ¼ cup more of sugar
¾ cup sugar	
1 cup water (or ¾ cup water; ¼ cup orange curaçao)	⅛ teaspoon salt
	1 nine inch baked pastry shell, cooled (buy one)

Wash and stem the berries. Save out 1 cup of the least perfect ones to make a glaze, as follows:

Glaze:

Cook 1 cup berries with sugar and water for 5 minutes. Strain. Mix a few tablespoons of the juice with the corn-starch-sugar mix. Add salt. Combine with rest of liquid in a small saucepan. Heat, stirring, until thick. This will take about 10 minutes. Cool. While the glaze is cooling, arrange the whole berries in the pie shell. Pour over the cooled glaze. Chill before serving. Serve the way it is, or pass a bowl of whipped cream to put on top. The pie is too pretty to cover.

Variation:

Berry-cheese pie. Soften 3 ounces of cream cheese with 1 tablespoon cream. Spread over pie shell before arranging the berries.

OLD-FASHIONED HOLIDAY DINNER
(WITH SOME NEW FLAVORS)

This menu was designed to let you have your holiday and enjoy it, too. Not that there's not a fair amount of cooking to do. But you can make the pie the day before; buy the onions, turnips and cranberry sauce ready prepared; and the method of not bothering with stuffing the bird makes the cooking much easier—(plus the dang old Bourbon gives you a beautifully moist flavorsome fowl and the recipe doesn't work when you stuff the bird.)

*Mulled Wine Soup**
*Bourbon Roast Chicken or Turkey**
*Cookie Sheet Stuffing (simply your favorite stuffing, or a pack-
    aged mix spread in a cookie sheet with sides and baked.
    Spread out into two sheets for a crisp stuffing; pile high
    onto one for a moister stuffing).*
Boiled Onions
Mashed Turnips (buy frozen)
Cranberry Sauce
*No-Cook Pumpkin Pie**
Coffee
*Leftovers: Turkey Puff**

Mulled Wine Soup

1½ cups claret wine
1 cinnamon stick (2 inches)
1 tablespoon sugar
4 cups beef consommé (2
    cans condensed beef

consommé plus water to
    make 4 cups; or
    packaged beef broth)
Lemon slices

Combine the claret, cinnamon stick and sugar in a sauce-pan; simmer 10 minutes. Stir in the consommé; heat *just* to boiling. Garnish with lemon slices. Good chilled, too. Serves 6.

Bourbon Roast Chicken (or Turkey)

2 four- to five-pound roasting
    chickens or a 12-pound
    turkey (this is not a
    good recipe for a larger
    turkey, as the bird is too

big to handle. If need
    be, try it with 2 turkeys)
Salt, pepper
¾ pound sweet butter
1 cup bourbon

Preheat your oven to 500° F. Wash and dry the birds well, patting the insides dry with paper towels. Sprinkle the insides with salt and pepper, and insert ¼ pound of sweet butter into each cavity. Truss birds with heavy string.

Place the chickens side by side, breast side up, in a large casserole or roasting pan. Salt and pepper them, and dot with more butter. Place, uncovered, in the very hot oven to brown. When the breasts are browned, turn and brown on the other side. This will take about 12–15 minutes.

Remove the pan from the oven and put it on top of the stove. Warm the bourbon and pour over the chickens. Light it and let it flame until the flames die down. Baste the chickens thoroughly with the resulting sauce. Put them breast side up, and cover the breasts lightly with foil to keep the chickens moist during the rest of the cooking.

Now turn down your oven to 325° and roast the chickens slowly. Baste and turn them occasionally, keeping the foil covering. (It is not necessary to turn a turkey.) Use two wooden spoons to turn the birds so you don't pierce the skin and let the juices escape. Cooking time will be about 25 minutes per pound (count weight of heaviest chicken) or about 2 hours after you start roasting at 325° F.

When ready to serve, keep the birds warm on a serving platter. Set the roasting pan on top of the stove and heat the juices left in the pan. Skim off the fat, and make either clear gravy or sour cream sauce.

Clear gravy:

Boil up the chicken livers, necks and gizzards in 2 cups of water while the chickens are roasting. Add sliced carrot, celery and onion and let simmer until the broth is reduced to 1 cup. Add this broth to the juices in the roasting pan, stir while heating, and strain into a gravy boat.

Sour cream bourbon sauce:

To the juices in the roasting pan, whisk in 1 cup sour cream, slowly. Stir constantly with a wire whisk or a wooden spoon over a low flame. Add 2 tablespoons bourbon, salt and pepper to taste. Keep stirring until the mixture reduces and thickens slightly. Serve.

No-Cook Pumpkin Pie

22 vanilla wafers or
  gingersnaps, two-inch
  round
1 pint vanilla ice cream,
  softened
1 can (1 pound) pumpkin
1¾ cups sugar
½ teaspoon ginger
½ teaspoon salt
1 teaspoon cinnamon
¼ teaspoon cloves
1 teaspoon vanilla extract
1½ cups heavy cream
1 cup slivered blanched
  almonds

Line a 10-inch pie pan with cookies. Spread ice cream over cookies. Freeze until firm. Mix pumpkin with 1½ cups of the sugar, salt, spices and vanilla. Whip 1 cup of the cream until stiff. Fold into pumpkin mixture. Pour over ice cream. Cover with foil. Freeze until firm, about 4 hours.

Meanwhile, combine slivered almonds with remaining ¼ cup sugar in a small skillet. Place over low heat, stirring quickly as sugar begins to turn color. Remove from heat when almonds are caramel colored. Spread on waxed paper or greased baking sheet. Break almonds apart when cool. Garnish pie with remaining ½ cup cream, whipped, and almonds. Serves 8.

Turkey Puff

3 cups diced cooked turkey
  (or chicken)
1 cup diced celery
1 medium onion, minced
½ cup mayonnaise
1 teaspoon salt
10 slices firm or stale bread
4 eggs
3 cups milk
2 cans (10½ ounces each)
  condensed cream of
  mushroom soup,
  undiluted
1 cup grated Cheddar cheese
Chopped parsley

Mix the first 5 ingredients. Cut the crusts from 6 slices of the bread and reserve. Cut the crusts and the remaining bread in ½ inch dice and put in a shallow 2½ quart baking dish. Cover with the turkey mixture. Cut the 6 bread slices in half to form triangles and arrange on top. Beat eggs and milk together and pour over mixture, being careful to cover the bread on top. Let stand in refrigerator several hours or overnight.

1 hour and 20 minutes before eating: Bake in 375° oven for 15 minutes. Remove from oven. Pour the soup over the top and sprinkle with cheese. Bake in a slow oven (325°) 1 hour, or until firm and golden brown. Sprinkle with parsley. Serves 6–8.

A WINTER COOK-IN DINNER

What could be more fun than to give a summer's barbecue dinner in the middle of a blizzard? This is a menu to spring on friends during the usual midwinter glumps.

The Cook-In Steaks are simply your favorite steaks cooked in the fireplace. You need a flat grill to set over wood or charcoal. Inexpensive ones can be bought for this purpose and used all winter. Or improvise a grill. You could use your oven grill propped up on bricks (with foil; slits between the bars for the air to get through. This saves a lot of cleaning later).

If you don't have a fireplace, try a hibachi near an open back door. Or use your summer barbecue grill outdoors. A little snow never hurt a good charcoal fire.

The Gratin and the Apple Crumble can be assembled in the morning and finished at dinner.

Hot Clam Broth (served in mugs and doctored with white wine,
    if you like)
Cook-In Steaks (discussed below)
Gratin Dauphinois*
Tossed Green Salad with Fruit (see Index)
Brandied Apple Crumble*
Coffee

Gratin Dauphinois

This method of slowly baking sliced potatoes in a sauce is nice because you can prepare the gratin in the morning, bake while you're doing other things. As my French mentor said facetiously as we were discussing Dauphinois, "of course you can make a lower calorie version by using bouillon instead of cream." You can. Up the garlic slightly.

2 pounds potatoes, peeled and sliced thinly
1½ cups gruyère cheese, grated
2 cups milk (or half and half if you really want to shoot the moon)

1 egg, well beaten
3½ tablespoons butter
Garlic, salt, pepper and nutmeg to taste

Arrange the potatoes in an oven-proof casserole. Mix the egg, milk and cheese. Season to taste. Pour over the potatoes. Dot with butter. Bake very slowly, 325°, covered, for 2 hours. Uncover the last 15 minutes. Serves 4–6.

Brandied Apple Crumble

This is our favorite cold-weather dessert. Assemble in the morning; bake it during cocktail hour; let it sit in the oven during dinner to cool slightly, and serve warm with brandied whipped cream, ice cream, hard sauce, or all by itself.

6 to 8 McIntosh apples
1 cup light brown sugar
½ teaspoon nutmeg
½ teaspoon cinnamon

½ teaspoon salt
1 tablespoon lemon juice
¼ cup brandy

Crumble topping:
¾ cup unsifted flour
½ cup sugar
1½ sticks of softened butter (⅜ pound)

1 teaspoon vanilla extract

Peel and core the apples; cut them into chunks into a deepish bowl. Sprinkle over the brown sugar, nutmeg, cinnamon, salt and lemon juice. Warm the brandy, pour over the apples and ignite. When the flames have died down, pour the apples into a shallow buttered baking dish. With your fingers, work the flour, sugar, butter and vanilla together until it holds its shape. Spread the topping over the apples. You can do this much ahead of time. Bake 50–60 minutes at 300°. Serves 6–8.

TOO-HOT-TO-COOK PARTIES

You almost always have to "cook" something, but there's no reason to be standing over a hot barbecue on a sweltering July night. Whatever needs cooking in these menus can be done the day before, or in the morning. Which means you can spend the afternoon swimming and still have thirty people wondering how you did it.

Salad-Bar Party

This is the kind of party that lends itself to being served in stages in different places. You could serve the bullshots in mugs while everybody's standing outdoors watching the sunset. Then stroll in to your salad bar set up in your dining area. Later, bring out the Fondue and coffee.

Bullshots (see index)
Make-Your-Own-Salad Bar*
Hot Loaves*
Crocks of sweet butter
Cheeses—Brie, Reblechon, Gjetost
Wine
and if you feel naked without more calories
A platter of boughten pastries or Chocolate Fondue*
Coffee

Make-Your-Own-Salad Bar

Help-yourself salad bars are as popular in California as they have ever been in France, where a Salad Composée has always been a thrifty way of using up hodge-podge and calling it dinner.

Salad-bar entertaining can be a welcome and easy change. You can use the idea as part of your menu (such as sliced steak and salad bar), or, with enough variety, the entire buffet party.

The main ingredients:

A large bowl of undressed crisp green, torn into bite-sized pieces

A choice of salad dressings
Bowls of accompaniments

The suggestions below can be enlarged, extended, changed, what have you, to suit the number of people and the style of your meal. (I once did this as a buffet dinner for 36 people, and included enough seafood not to feel guilty that it was so easy.)

The salad greens (choose an assortment):

Romaine lettuce
Iceberg lettuce
Boston lettuce
Chicory
Escarole

Spinach
Dandelion greens
Arrugala (a spicy Italian lettuce)

If the size of your party and your table permits, arrange the greens down the center in separate bowls. The important thing is to wash and crisp them long enough ahead so the greens are really crisp. (An easy method is to fill the sink up with cold water. Separate all the leaves and let the greens take a bath. Drain onto paper towels. Wrap in a clean dish towel and chill. See "Have Food, Will Travel," page 20.)

Bowls of accompaniments:

Surround the bowls of greens with small bowls of any or all of the following:
Anchovy fillets
Artichoke hearts
Broccoli and cauliflower flowerets
Cheese—fresh grated Parmesan or Romano
Cold sliced chicken
Cold cooked shrimp
Crabmeat or ham

Garlic croutons
Green beans, cooked and marinated in Vinaigrette (see Index)
Hearts of palm
Sliced cucumbers
Sliced fresh mushrooms
Sliced green and red peppers
Sliced olives
Sliced onion rings
Tomato wedges
Tongue in julienne strips

Salad Dressings
You should have a choice of at least three in pitchers or bowls at the end of the table.

Cruets of oil and vinegar
Vinaigrette dressing (see Index)
Creamy blue cheese dressing

Russian dressing
Mayonnaise ravigote (see Index)

Hot Loaves

The simplest ever is just to heat loaves of unsliced bread. Serve them on a wooden board. Pass a crock of sweet butter. White, rye, black bread—you start to taste the bread when it's warm.

Chocolate Fondue

The fondue sauce:
9 bars of Swiss milk chocolate (the kind with honey and almonds), or any milk chocolate candy bars.

1½ cups heavy cream or milk
6 tablespoons kirsch

In a small chafing dish, or a fondue pan, melt the chocolate with the cream over a very low fire. Stir in the kirsch.

What you dip with: Fresh fruit (chunks of pineapple, orange sections, ripe pears); Chunks of angel-food cake; Small meringues; And/or miniature cream puffs.

To eat: Arrange fruit and cake chunks around the fondue pan. Use fondue forks or skewers or long toothpicks. Spear a piece of fruit or cake and dip it into the warm chocolate sauce. Serves 12.

Dirty Old Steak Party

Eliminating appetizers always makes me feel less guilty about putting the money into steak. And men love sliced steak so—plus the cheese cake is great, and filling—that it's worth it. Particularly for an après-sailing or waterskiing day.

You can handle cooking the steaks like this: if you know you're giving this party, the next time you barbecue cook all your steaks for the party and freeze them. Or do them the afternoon before. (See "Cook Double" page 20.)

The cake can be made the day before, and the vegetable casserole keeps for at least a week in the refrigerator. So hope it rains the morning before the party and you can get all your cooking done.

> *Sliced Steak Sandwiches**
> *Cold Mustard Sauce**
> *Armenian Vegetable Casserole**
> *Chocolate Cheese Cake**

Sliced Steak Sandwiches

Cold Sliced Steak You Can Prepare Ahead of Time:
Use beef tenderloin, or shells of beef (if you own tax exempts). Broil or grill them (as suggested above) for *slightly less time* than the way you like them. The meat will continue cooking as it cools. Then refrigerate overnight or freeze.

To serve: Bring the steaks to room temperature. Slice them and place on warmed, never toasted, buttered rye bread or rolls or French bread.

Hot Sliced Steak Sandwiches

You can, of course, center your party around an outdoor grill and make it an Almost-Too-Hot-To-Cook Party. Cook your steaks, slice and serve them hot. Or try this quick method.

Mini-wiches (which are also great as an appetizer)
Slice raw beefsteak into thin slices (ask your butcher to do this on his ham slicer, or get the meat good and cold and then slice). Butter French rolls. Cut into quarters. Warm in foil. Grill the beef slices quickly, a few at a time, over barbecue or hibachi. It won't take more than a minute. Cut them to fit the bread. Salt and pepper. Serve.

Cold Mustard Sauce (for Cold Sliced Steak)

1 cup mayonnaise
2 teaspoons prepared Dijon mustard
2 teaspoons Rose's Lime Juice

Beat the mustard and juices into the mayonnaise.

Armenian Vegetable Casserole

Here is a cross between a ratatouille and vegetables *à la grecque*. Serve at room temperature.

2 cups olive oil approximately
1 cup eggplant, unpeeled, cut into 1-inch cubes
2 tomatoes, sliced ½ inch thick
1 cup zucchini, cut into ½-inch slices
1 cup green pepper, cut in 1-inch rings
1 large onion, sliced and separated into rings
1 cup celery, cut into 1-inch slices
1 cup shredded cabbage
1 cup green beans, cut into 1-inch slices
1 cup carrots, cut into ¼-inch slices
1 cup white seedless grapes
Salt and pepper
4 cloves garlic, sliced
2 cups chopped parsley
1 teaspoon oregano
1 teaspoon basil
½ teaspoon crumbled bay leaf
1 teaspoon sugar

Use a large casserole. Pour a little olive oil into it. Make individual layers of all the vegetables and the grapes, seasoning each layer with salt, pepper, garlic, parsley, oregano, basil, bay leaf, and a little olive oil. Use the sugar on the layers of tomato. Make the top layer an assortment of all the vegetables and the grapes.

Bake uncovered in a 350° F. oven for 1½ hours, or till oil is bubbling and vegetables are completely tender. Serve at room temperature.

This will keep in the refrigerator for at least a week. Serves 8 as vegetable; 12–15 as appetizer.

Chocolate Cheese Cake

This may only be the best cheese cake you've ever tasted—and well worth the effort of dragging a springform pan (the baking pan whose sides spring open) to your second house. Or make it at home. It tastes good two and three days later, if it lasts that long.

Vanilla wafer crumbs to line a 9-inch spring form pan (Mix crumbs with ⅓ cup melted butter)	½ cup hot strong coffee 1 teaspoon vanilla ⅛ teaspoon salt 1 pound cream cheese
2 packages (6 ounces each) chocolate bits	4 eggs, separated ⅔ cup sugar

Beat the egg yolks with half of the sugar until light and lemony. Melt the chocolate bits with the coffee in a double boiler. Add vanilla and salt.

Cool slightly and beat in the softened cream cheese. Stir in the egg yolk mixture. Beat the egg whites with the remaining sugar until stiff. Fold in. Pour into a crumb-lined springform pan. Bake at 350° for 1 hour. Allow the cake to stay in the oven until cool. Serves 6–8.

BIG CHEAP NO-COOK REVENGE PARTY

The time comes where you owe everybody and you'd like to get even. A cocktail party won't get you off the hook. A dinner party is too much trouble.

You want to do something big and cheap and be done with it. Yet, with a little style.

This menu takes some advance marketing and assembling, but no cooking, and nothing to do at the party, so you could manage quite a crowd with no help at all.

> *Make-Your-Own Hero Sandwiches**
> *Cherry Tomatoes—Celery and Carrot Sticks*
> *Beer and Ale*
> *Biscuit Tortoni—Espresso Coffee*

All the fixings for the heros get spread out on a large table looking very impressive. You buy the tortoni and use wooden spoons to eat it with. Serve indoors or out, noon or night.

Make-Your-Own Hero Sandwiches

The nice thing about this kind of buffet is you can serve up to dozens of people, simply adding more of anything you want.

Your heroes and heroines are then free to assemble their own sandwiches, competing with each other as to who can invent the most fanciful combinations.

Your buffet table should be arranged with the foods in the order they are assembled (left to right, or right to left depending on how you feel about it).

Breads

Individual Italian hero loaves, split in half lengthwise, or use large loaves, split in half. Keep a loaf at a time on a long wooden board, with a knife. Your guests can lop off as large a hero as they like.

* Recipe follows

Mayonnaise

A bowl of mayonnaise mixed with chopped fresh parsley to spread on the bottom of the sandwich.

Meats

It is best to buy your meats where you can have them sliced very thinly on a machine. The thinness is what gives the sandwich its character. Arrange one or more kinds of meat on platters: Genoa Salami, Prosciutto ham, Bologna, Pepperoni, Italian sausages, Roast beef (if you want to splurge), Spiced ham, Sliced Tongue, Mortadella.

Cheeses

Arrange thin slices of these cheeses on platters: Provolone, Swiss cheese, American cheese, Gorgonzola, Mozzarella.

Garnishes

Next in order should come bowls and platters with various garnishes to spoon or lay on top of sandwiches: Shredded lettuce (lots of it), Onion rings, Whole anchovies, Slices of pimentoes, Thinly sliced tomatoes, Green and red peppers (Sauté them in olive oil with sliced onion until they are just tender).

Finishing Touches

The final stroke of heroism is to douse the entire sandwich with as much as you like of oil, vinegar and seasonings. Have these handy: Cruets of olive oil and wine vinegar, Dried oregano, Grated Parmesan cheese.

BIG EXPENSIVE NO-COOK WINE TASTING

Sometimes you want to pull out all the stops and create a zap! drop dead! afternoon or evening for any number of people. Still, you don't want to paint up the garage and pretend it's a gazebo (as someone we know did). Nor do you want to hire a caterer complete with tent (which fell down at one beach house deck party we went to). Nor do you want to go to the trouble of moving all the furniture out of the cottage so there's room for tables (the last time I did that, it rained!).

Victor, the extraordinary sommellier of the Brussels restaurant in New York City, came to our rescue when we invented a wine-tasting as the solution to handling over a hundred people. He helped us decide that three kinds of wine were all we could handle for that large a crowd. And so we started with:

A red Bordeaux—St. Emilion

A red Burgundy—Vosnes Romanée

A German White—Sturmburger

plus rented wine glasses, three times the number of people. We opened a few bottles of each wine at a time and clustered them with glasses along a sideboard. People helped themselves.

On a buffet table, using wooden boards for everything and baskets for the breads we had:

Cheeses: Brie, Fontina, Reblechon, Appenzel, Stilton, Gjetost, Ricotta Romano, Caccio Cavallo, Gourmandise (An assortment, creamy, semi-soft, and hard)

Meats: Coppa di Piacenza (an Italian Prosciutto-like ham), *Citterio* (Milanese Salami), Westphalian Ham, Pâté (a homemade pâté made by a local specialty store), *Sopressata* (an Italian, no-garlic salami), *Pepperoni* (hot, spicy sausage), Italian sweet sausages

Breads: Thin French breads (heated and sliced into ½-inch slices), Thin rye bread, Pumpernickel bread, Genoa toast, Assorted crackers.

Fruits (our centerpiece was of edible fruit): Comice pears, Apples, Grapes

And Accompaniments—Crocks of sweet butter, scattered among the cheeses, Assorted mustards, Bowl of nuts, Bowl of dried figs, Bowl of olives.

Lest you feel you have to mortgage your second house to

duplicate this menu, I should point out that you don't need a large amount of any of the foods. The sheer variety, spread out on the table—small amounts of many different things—is what creates the ambience. Plus, of course, the wine.

A wine-tasting can extend over an afternoon with friends dropping in and out. Or provide an evening's entertainment. Or be a Holiday Open House. The only real trick, aside from the shopping, is to check with your cheese store to find out how long each cheese should stand at room temperature before serving. With Brie, for example, the time out will depend on its feel at the time you buy it. It should be soft to the point of runny.

SAME FOOD, NEW FACES

(*Several Parties on the Same Weekend*)

Sometimes everybody you know is going to be out, or up, that weekend. Not visiting you, but in the area. You'd love to have one couple for dinner; perhaps a few others for lunch; or a small spontaneous dinner party. That's all very ambitious, but how do you get out of the kitchen to talk to anybody?

We invented this style out of need, one weekend, not knowing how we'd feel about eating the same food repeatedly. But it ended up being enormous fun—people in and out—food appearing—we, relaxed, not at all bored by seeing the same ham bow in and bow out—a little shorter each time.

The concept that evolved was why not cook a lot of a good meat and keep serving it hot or cold while changing the accompaniments (which don't take all that much time to fix). It's something like wearing a basic dress, changing the accessories to suit the occasion. The dress has got to be good.

The Same-Ham Plan

We started with a 10-pound boneless ham. Here's what happened.

DINNER FOR FOUR (ON A FRIDAY NIGHT):

> *Braised Ham in Madeira Sauce**
> *Sautéed Mushroom Caps*
> *Tossed Green Salad*
> *Hot Rolls and Butter*
> *Cold Lemon Mousse**
> *Coffee*

SATURDAY AFTERNOON LUNCH FOR SIX:

The same Ham, cold and sliced—The same Madeira Sauce, cold
*Hot or Cold Potato Salad**
*Russian Eggplant Caviar** (*served on lettuce as a salad*)
Hot Rye Bread—Herb Butter
*Melon Surprise**
Coffee

SUPPER FOR SIX THAT SUNDAY EVENING:

The same Ham, cold and sliced—The same Madeira Sauce, cold
The rest of the Eggplant Caviar
Tomato and Onion Salad
Hot French Bread—Butter
Coffee and Cookies

SUPPER FOR SIX (TWO WEEKS LATER, AFTER FREEZING
THE REMAINDER):

> *The same Ham in Hot Ham Sandwiches**
> *Sliced tomatoes*

That first weekend, I did most of the cooking for all the meals while the ham was braising. The afternoon's cooking produced the Eggplant Caviar, the Cold Lemon Mousse a~ the Melon Surprise. Needless to say, the rest of the wee' was a breeze and produced at least three invitations to other people's houses where, luckily, we did not find the same ham.

The Same Other Foods

You can have a "Same Food, New Faces" weekend using

Fillet of beef
Roast Beef
Whole Roasted Chickens

Chicken Breasts
Lamb

Ham Braised in Madeira Sauce

1 cup sliced onions
1 cup sliced carrots
2 tablespoons butter
1 tablespoon oil
An 8 to 10-pound cooked ham or picnic shoulder, skinned and trimmed of excess fat (try a boned rolled ham which makes for a marvelous slicing)
2 cups Madeira wine
3 cups stock or canned beef bouillon
6 parsley sprigs
1 bay leaf
½ teaspoon thyme

Sauce
3 tablespoons arrowroot (or 2 tablespoons flour; or 1 tablespoon cornstarch)
2 tablespoons cold stock or wine
½ cup mushrooms, diced and sautéed

Will serve 16–20 all at once or at different times.

To cook ahead: Use a heavy covered roaster, or casserole, just large enough to hold the ham. Cook the vegetables in butter and oil in the roaster until lightly browned. Place the ham in the roaster, pour in the wine, the stock or bouillon, and add the herbs. Bring to a simmer on top of the stove, cover, and bake very slowly (325° oven) for 2 to 2½ hours, basting every 20 minutes.

Pour off the liquid from ham into a saucepan. Skim the grease off the top, and boil it down rapidly to make 3 cups.

Strain it into another saucepan. Blend the arrowroot with
the cold liquid and beat it into the hot braising liquid. Stir
in the mushrooms. Simmer for 5 minutes. Correct the seasoning.

Cold Lemon Mousse

This is a summer's delight. Best made the day before to let
the texture develop, and worth the beating time.

1 tablespoon gelatin   ½ cup sugar
2 tablespoons water   5 eggs, separated
Juice and grated zest of 2   1 cup heavy cream
  lemons
¼ cup Sake (or a sweet
  white wine)

Sprinkle the gelatin over the water. In a small double boiler
combine the lemon juice and grated zest, sugar and Sake.
Heat. Add the gelatin mix and stir until the gelatin and sugar
are dissolved. Beat the egg yolks until they are light and
lemony color. Stir in the lemon gelatin mixture.
  Beat the egg whites stiff. Fold them into the yolk mixture.
Chill 30 minutes to an hour until the mousse is cold but not
set. Whip ½ cup of the heavy cream, adding a bit of sugar
just before the cream is set. Fold the whipped cream into
the mousse.
  Chill overnight (or at least 4 hours) in a bowl or mold.
You can freeze this, too, and serve frozen. Serve accompa-
nied by a bowl of the rest of the cream, whipped lightly, to
spoon over the top.

Hot or Cold Potato Salad

This is a delicious European-style potato salad, which you
can heat or chill. To Americanize it, just add mayonnaise,
but I think it's better the way it is.

10 boiled potatoes
¼ cup dry vermouth or white
   wine
¼ cup chicken bouillon
1 bunch scallions, finely
   chopped (use almost all
   the tops)

5 tablespoons chopped
   parsley
½ cup to ¾ cup vinaigrette
   (depending on the
   mealiness of the
   potatoes) see recipe,
   page 157

Boil the potatoes in their jackets until they are just tender.
Peel them hot and slice them into a large bowl. Pour over
the vermouth and bouillon, and toss gently. Let the potatoes
stand as long as possible (2 hours or more) to absorb the
liquid. Toss gently now and then. Add the scallions, parsley,
and vinaigrette, and toss again. Chill to serve hot. Heat in a
covered saucepan over a low flame to serve hot. Serves 8–10.

Russian Eggplant Caviar

This can be made a day or two ahead of time.

1 large, or two medium
   eggplants
2 onions, chopped fine
2 tomatoes, chopped
2 cloves garlic, crushed
1 teaspoon sugar

2 tablespoons lemon juice
3 tablespoons olive oil
Olive oil for sautéing
Salt and pepper
Chopped parsley
Sour cream for garnish

Place the eggplant in a pan, and bake until soft, about 30
minutes. Remove the skin and chop the eggplant fine. In a
small amount of olive oil, sauté the onions and garlic quickly,
just until the onions are heated through but not browned.
Add the tomatoes, eggplant, and seasonings. (You'll need a
lot of salt—at least 2 teaspoons.) Mix well, but don't heat.
Chill the mix in a covered container. It will keep for several
days. Serves 6.

To serve as a salad: Stir through 2–3 tablespoons chopped
parsley just before serving. Spoon onto lettuce cups on individual salad plates. Top each serving with a dollop of sour
cream.

To serve as an appetizer: A bowl full of Russian eggplant caviar makes a delicious appetizer for another time. Serve with black bread and a bowl of sour cream on the side. Each guest spreads the caviar on a slice of bread, tops with a dollop of sour cream.

Melon Surprises

There are several fun things you can do to melons, all of which are worth considering because you can do it to them the day before and get dessert out of the way. The number of servings will depend on the size of the melon.

Watermelon Ginny

A large watermelon, or   1 bottle gin
    "sugar baby"

You plug the watermelon in 3 spots. Dig in with a melon scoop to remove some of the fruit to make room for the gin. Pour ⅓ of the gin into each opening. Replace the plugs, sealing with tape. Refrigerate overnight.

Serve, simply sliced. Or make melon balls to add to a fruit bowl.

Honeydew Surprise

1 large honeydew melon   ½ cup blueberries
1 package black raspberry
    gelatin

Make up the black raspberry gelatin according to the package directions. Chill until almost jelled.

Cut a slice off the stem end of the honeydew. Reach in with a long handled spoon and scoop out all the seeds. Wash the melon in cold water to remove any stray seeds.

Mix the blueberries into the chilled gelatin. Spoon into the honeydew cavity. Refrigerate until set.

Serve by cutting the melon into wedges.

Note: A nice, and perhaps easier, variation with smaller melons or cantaloupes is simply to cut them in half, allowing half a melon per person. Fill with the fruity gelatin.

Melon Compote

Another fun way of using melon is to cut off one end, as in the Honeydew Surprise, above. Scoop out melon balls, emptying the entire shell. Be careful not to pierce the skin. Mix the melon balls with your favorite fresh fruit. Repack into the melon. Pour over gin or kirsch or champagne to fill. Replace the lid and seal. Serves 4–6.

The Ham Again

Hot Ham Sandwiches

1 cup milk	2 eggs
8 slices day old bread	¼ cup olive oil
8 slices cooked lean ham	Salt and pepper

Put the milk in a shallow dish. Dip each slice of bread in until the bread is damp, but not soaked.

Fold each piece of bread over a slice of ham, and weight the sandwiches under a bread board or anything flat and heavy you can find. Let them stand about half an hour. Beat the eggs with salt and pepper. Dip each sandwich in the egg mix and fry in hot olive oil until well browned. Serves 4.

NIBBLERS AND GOBBLERS
Cocktail-Buffet Dinner Parties

Nibblers and gobblers is the name for a style we had to invent when we wanted to give a large party for the marital merger of two talented friends. Documentary film producer Gordon Hyatt is a gobbler. He likes a lot of food. His bride, Carole Frimith Schwartz, who created the Child Research Service, Inc., was and is a nibbler. Carole likes to nibble from a table all evening long.

From that came our Nibbler and Gobbler merger of the cocktail party with the dinner party. It's wonderful. You just keep everything on the table all night and eat when you feel like it. Those who want appetizers with their drinks can start early. The serious drinkers can wait. As host or hostess, you're free to mingle, and nibble or gobble as you will. You can serve dessert as an aftermath late in the evening. Or have an electric coffeepot and your dessert fixings right there to one side.

The Original Nibblers and Gobblers Menu
(for 50 People)

To nibble:

A large block of pâté, served with rye bread rounds and butter.

Cucumber salad (nibbled with toothpicks or gobbled with a fork on the dinner plate).

Cheeses, served with hot sliced French bread, kept warm in a serving basket.

Cold shrimp in dill served with dilled mayonnaise. Toothpicks to spear with.

To gobble:

Marzetti* kept warm in two large chafing dishes.

Midnight Dessert

Chocolate Mousse icebox cake*
Coffee

   * Recipe follows

Marzetti

An easy and delicious hamburger-noodle bake for a care-free party buffet. It doubles, triples or octuples just fine.

1 pound ground chuck
1 pound ground veal
2 tablespoons olive oil
1 large onion, chopped
⅔ cup chopped green
    pepper
2 8-ounce cans sliced
    mushrooms, drained
1½ teaspoons salt
½ teaspoon pepper
1 teaspoon oregano

2 cans (8 ounces) sauce
    Arturo or tomato soup
1 can (6 ounces) tomato
    paste
⅔ cup water
2 tablespoons Worcestershire
    sauce
8 ounces broad noodles
½ pound shredded sharp
    cheese

To cook ahead: Brown meat in shortening in a heavy skillet. Add onion, green pepper, mushrooms, and seasonings. Cook until tender, about 5 minutes. Combine with sauce Arturo, tomato paste, water, and Worcestershire sauce.

Cook noodles in boiling water until almost tender; drain and rinse.

In a large, greased baking dish, spread half of noodles, cover with half of meat and sauce mixture, and sprinkle with half of cheese; repeat, using remaining ingredients.

45 minutes before eating: Bake in a moderate oven (375°) or until heated. Serves 8.

Chocolate Mousse Icebox Cake

You can double or triple this easily for a party and there's never any left over. But it does take more time than some of my other desserts.

½ pound semi-sweet chocolate
2 tablespoons strong coffee
2 tablespoons brandy
4 eggs (separated)

1 cup confectioners' sugar
1 teaspoon vanilla
Pinch of salt
Macaroons (½ to ¾ pound)

Melt the chocolate with coffee and brandy in double boiler. Add well-beaten egg yolks and sugar and cook slowly until smooth, stirring constantly. Cool, add vanilla, and fold in lightly the stiffly beaten whites.

Line a large glass bowl with macaroons; fill with chocolate mixture and cover top with macaroons. Let stand several hours in refrigerator, or overnight. Serve, garnished with whipped cream. Serves 4–5.

Mexican Smorgasbord

To nibble:

Guacamole served with corn chips*
Shrimp
Bowl of pepitas
Bowl of plantain chips (French fried banana chips you
    can buy)
Margaritas to drink (see Index)

To gobble:

Hot bean dip*—corn chips
Posole (page 133)
    (Double or triple the recipe using the larger amount of
    pork)

For dessert:

Help-yourself strawberries*

Guacamole

Chunky, creamy, hot-spicy, or not so—the styles of guacamole depend entirely on your taste. This version can be "hottened up" or cooled down, by increasing or going easy on the chili powder and Tabasco.

2 ripe avocados
1 onion, chopped
2 teaspoons chili powder
3 teaspoons chili sauce
   (which I like better than chopped tomatoes

because the mix gets less watery. However, you can substitute 1 chopped tomato, if you prefer.)
4 dashes Tabasco sauce
1 teaspoon lemon juice

Peel and pit the avocados. Mash them well. Add the finely chopped onion, and other ingredients to taste. (If you make it ahead of time, put the pits back into the mix to keep it from darkening.)

1. *As a dip:* These accompaniments go well with guacamole: cooked, cold shrimp on toothpicks, corn chips, Japaleno Sauce (a canned sauce of hot chilis, of which a little bit on top goes a long way. El Paso is the brand to look for), peeled green peppers, raw cauliflower, shredded lettuce, tortilla chips, tostados.

2. *As a salad:* Stuff scooped-out tomatoes with guacamole. Serve on a bed of shredded lettuce.

3. *As a main course:* Spread guacamole over cold sliced cooked fish.

Hot Mexican Bean Dip

A delicious and unusual filler-upper.

1 can (1 pound 10 ounces)
   pork and beans; or chili and beans
½ cup American cheese
1 teaspoon garlic salt
1 teaspoon chili powder
½ teaspoon salt
Dash pepper

2 teaspoons Worcestershire sauce
½ teaspoon liquid smoke (optional)
4 slices crumbled bacon for garnish
Corn chips to dip with

If you have a blender, blend all the ingredients except bacon and corn chips until smooth. Taste for seasoning. Transfer to the top of a double boiler or a chafing dish. Heat before serving. Top with crumbled bacon and use the corn chips to dip with.

Without a blender, force the beans through a strainer into your cooking pan. Grate the cheese. Mix in the other ingredients. Heat. Serves 6 to 8 as appetizer dip.

Variations: Try this with canned black beans. Add a little sour cream.

Help-Yourself Strawberries

This is a nice way to handle a party buffet for a crowd. You don't have to spend all that time standing over strawberry hulls.

2 quarts strawberries, washed just before the party, and drained quickly but unhulled and left whole	2 packages (8 ounces each) cream cheese ¼ cup light brown sugar 1 teaspoon ground cinnamon

Form softened cream cheese into a roll. Combine the brown sugar and cinnamon and sprinkle over the roll.

To serve: Arrange the cheese roll on a tray, surrounded by the whole strawberries. People slice a bit of cheese to spread on a strawberry for finger-food. Or provide small plates to hold a chunk of cheese with several berries. Serves 8.

Antipasto Con Pasta

To nibble:

Chick peas remoulade*
Italian sausages & salami
Marinated mushrooms (page 108)
Olives
Prosciutto & melon (small bits of melon wrapped in prosciutto and secured on individual toothpicks)
Sliced Italian bread

To gobble:

Spaghetti and Lobster Casserole*

Dessert:

Summer fruit bowl*

Chick Peas Remoulade

This is a good dish for an antipasto or a buffet appetizer. Try it as a salad, on a bed of lettuce.

2 anchovy fillets
1 clove garlic, crushed
1 tablespoon capers, chopped
1 teaspoon shallots, chopped
2 tablespoons parsley, chopped

½ cup mayonnaise
Salt, pepper
Lemon juice
1 can (✳2) chick peas

Blend first five ingredients into the mayonnaise, adding salt, pepper, and lemon juice to taste. Mix with the chick peas and refrigerate until well chilled. You can do this the day before. Serves 4–6 for appetizer.

Spaghetti and Lobster Casserole

Unlike some casseroles which are a lot of pasta with a little sauce, this one is a lot of sauce and less pasta.

3 pounds cooked lobster meat (Buy already prepared, or boil lobsters or lobster tails. It takes about 4 pounds of whole lobster to get 1 pound of meat; so it's really easier to buy the prepared.)
1 pound fine ✳9 spaghetti, boiled and drained or kept over hot water

1 pound butter
2 bottles ketchup
Worcestershire sauce to taste
Salt, pepper, dry mustard to taste
1 pound American cheese, grated
Bread crumbs

To cook ahead: Slice lobster into small chunks. Make sauce in a double boiler—melt the butter, add ketchup, Worcestershire sauce, salt, pepper, and dry mustard (to taste).

Butter one large or two small casseroles and place in layers: spaghetti, lobster, sauce, grated cheese. Repeat. Refrigerate until ready to bake.

45 minutes before eating: Sprinkle with bread crumbs. Bake at 350°. Serves 12.

Summer Fruit Bowl

This is good to do in the morning. Or make syrup ahead of time, and add to fruits on serving day.

2 cups water	1 small cantaloupe
1½ cups granulated sugar	2 oranges
3 tablespoons lemon juice	2 nectarines (or 4 apricots)
2 tablespoons anise seed	2 purple plums
½ teaspoon salt	1 cup seedless green grapes
1 small pineapple	1 lime, sliced
1 small honeydew melon	

In a medium saucepan, combine water with sugar, lemon juice, anise seed and salt. Cook over medium heat 15 minutes until mixture reaches light syrup consistency; chill in refrigerator.

Several hours ahead, peel pineapple, melon, cantaloupe and oranges and cut into bite-size chunks. Slice nectarines and plums in wedges. Combine the cut-up fruits with grapes and lime slices in a large serving bowl. Pour chilled syrup through strainer over fruits. Refrigerate, stirring occasionally. Serves 10–12.

PARTIES YOU PAY OTHER PEOPLE FOR

Sometimes you simply need to hire somebody else to provide your party.

Not all of the ideas below may be followable in every locale, but then again you may have some local specialty to tap from. The point is, why not scout your area for something other than the usual cook or caterer?

1. *Hire the Sabrett man.* We have local hot-dog trucks called "Sabrett." You can bargain with the driver to come and provide a hot-dog party. Pay for the amount your guests eat plus something for the driver.

2. *Find the local bread-bakers.* A bread-tasting makes a wonderful afternoon party. If you don't feel up to baking your own, or inviting guests to bring their specialties, look into the local bake shops. Chances are you can arrange to buy a variety of loaves. Breads, butter, cheeses and Margaritas to drink. You've got a party.

3. *Find someone who can make the well-known regional dish.* Often someone in the family or your local fish store or grocer has a special chowder or baked beans or bisque or whatever. Make that dish the highlight of your party . . . but taste before you order!

4. *Clam bake.* Caterers who specialize in clam bakes will come out and dig a pit near your house, and provide dinner for dozens of people.

5. *Call a local specialty restaurant.* Often a restaurant near house ✳2 will be happy to provide you with party foods, given enough notice. A good Japanese, Chinese, Mexican, Hawaiian, or French restaurant could give you the basis for an interesting foreign buffet table.

8

OUTDOORSMANSHIP:
Where the Mess is
outside (mostly)

"The sensuous stirrings in man and his mate when they are alone among trees, earth, and sea . . . have been replaced by the barbecue."

Jerome and Julie Rainer
Sexual Pleasure In Marriage*

* Reprinted by permission of Simon and Schuster, Inc.

Eating outdoors is as American as air pollution. And a natural way to entertain easily in your vacation house. But long before the $8.95 barbecue existed, other people in the world have been eating outdoors. Spanish field hands have built fires wherever they were—grilled fish on sticks—thrown eggplants and peppers into the coals to cook and char, then peeled them, sprinkling them with oil and salt, and eaten them. In the Argentine, they build fire pits in the ground to cook a sumptuous mixed grill called *asado* (lit. "roasted").

Almost every country has its characteristic style of outdoor eating, some of which I've sketched in the menus which follow. Outdoors can mean either at your house, or, with a little equipment, a picnic anywhere . . . beach, field, stream. And with so many serving aids on the market, almost any menu can transit from indoors to out.

(Some Outdoor Parties for Kids can be found in chapter 9, "Filling the Generation Gap.")

EIN AUSFLUG

In German forests and picnic areas, one sees signs tacked up to trees:

> Der alte Brauch wird nicht gebrochen
> Hier koennen Familien Kaffee kochen
> (No change in the old ways.
> Families can make coffee around here)

Picnic-bound families, or groups of young people on a day's excursion, carry baskets of the traditional Ausflug fare —sausages, cheese, and beer, stopping in the picnic areas to have coffee and Kuchen.

The Ausflug menu makes a fine American picnic. Or give a lunch and swimming party for as many as you like and set up an Ausflug buffet table.

Sausages, sliced only as you need them for sandwiches
Leberwurst
Blutwurst
Schwademagen
Cervelat
Salamie
Teewurst
Schinken
Bread—black bread or rye
Butter
Mustard
Cheese—Tilsitter and Muenster. Try Hand Käse if you can find it
Beer

Arrange the meats, cheese and bread and butter on platters. Heap the beer bottles into a tub of ice. Serve coffee and Kuchen later.

UNE FETE CHAMPETRE

Literally this means a feast in the fields, or, a picnic. But, as with ein Ausflug, there's no reason not to adapt the style and menu of a Fête Champêtre for an outdoor party buffet.

Cold Blender Vichyssoise (kept cold in a large ice bucket)
Poulet Tarragon, Froid* (cold tarragon chicken*) or Cold
*   Roasted Meat**
Salade de Pomme de Terre Français (hot or cold potato salad,
*   page 181)*
Green Beans Vinaigrette (optional—page 156)
Tomato and Onion Salad (optional)
French Bread—Butter
Cheese
Fruit
White Wine or Champagne

Blender Vichyssoise

4 cups peeled, diced raw
  potatoes
White part of 4 leeks, sliced
2 small onions, coarsely
  chopped
2 cups chicken consommé
1 teaspoon salt

¼ teaspoon pepper
½ teaspoon dill seed
2 cups milk
2 cups heavy cream
Chopped fresh dill or chives
  for garnish

To cook ahead: Blend the potatoes, leeks, onion, chicken consommé, salt, pepper and dill seed at high speed for 20 seconds. You'll have to do this in 2 or 3 stages, pouring out the blended mixture into a saucepan. When all the mix has been blended and in the pan, stir in milk. Bring to a boil, then simmer, covered, over low heat for 10 minutes, stirring often. Return part of soup to blender, filling container ¼ full. Cover and turn motor on high; remove cover and gradually pour in soup until the container is full. Pour the blended soup into a large bowl. Repeat with the unblended soup until finished. At this point, you can freeze the stock or keep refrigerated for a day.

Serving Day: Re-blend the thawed or chilled soup for 20 seconds. Pour into your serving bowl. Stir in the heavy cream. Chill until serving time; then garnish liberally with chopped dill or chives. Serves 8–10.

Cold Tarragon Chicken

This is one of the best ways to roast chicken to eat cold at a picnic or outdoor party.

3 three-pound chickens
Salt and freshly ground
  pepper to taste
6 sprigs fresh tarragon
3 cloves garlic, peeled

1½ bay leaves
¾ pound butter (3 sticks)
6 small white onions, peeled
3 carrots coarsely chopped

Preheat the oven to 450°. Sprinkle chickens inside and out with salt and pepper. Place two sprigs tarragon, one clove garlic, ½ bay leaf and ½ stick butter in the cavity of each chicken. Truss chickens with string or safety pins (see page 38).

Heat remaining butter in a large casserole on top of stove. Place chickens in a casserole and turn them in butter without browning. Scatter onions and carrots around chickens. Place the casserole in the oven and bake 15 minutes, basting the chickens occasionally. Turn chickens to other side and bake, basting, 15 minutes longer. Turn chickens on their backs and continue baking, basting, until they are golden brown, about 30 minutes. Total cooking time should be about one hour. When cooked, the chickens should be nicely browned and the liquid should run clear when the thigh is pierced with a fork.

Let chickens stand at room temperature until cool, then chill until ready to serve. Serves 9–10.

Cold Roasted Meat

Cold sliced beef for outdoors or a picnic is delicious. In addition to the Filet de Boeuf Froid, below, you can roast almost any boneless rolled piece of beef, or lamb. The secret is to cook it very rare, chill well, and slice thin.

To make sure it'll be rare, take your roast out of the oven 15–20 minutes *before* it is done. The meat will continue cooking as it cools.

Filet de Boeuf Froid

This is a drop-dead dish (either for your guests or your pocketbook). But worth having in your catalog for once-a-year occasions. And it's easy. At those prices, it should be. You can cook it ahead of time, or last minute.

5- to 6-pound filet of beef   Larding pork

Ask your butcher to trim away the fat and connective tissues and lard the filet with larding pork; or tie thin strips of fat salt pork or beef suet around it.

Place the roast on a rack in a shallow roasting pan in a preheated 450° oven and roast it for 35 to 40 minutes, or until a meat thermometer inserted in the heaviest part registers 125° for rare.

At this point, you can cool the meat and refrigerate a day, bringing it to room temperature before serving. Or, place on a serving platter and allow the meat to "rest" for about 20 minutes. Then slice fairly thin and garnish with a bouquet of fresh watercress.

Serve with toast and sauce Bearnaise which I buy, because that's where I draw the line come vacation but you can make it from any good French cookbook. Serves 6–8 if you really make thin slices.

EL DIA DE CAMPO

Eating in the open air (*el día de campo* means a day in the country, or a picnic), is one of the delights offered by the Spanish climate. This menu can travel, or stay right on your porch for party lunch or dinner.

Cold Gazpacho* (kept cold in an ice bucket)
Bowls of Accompaniments: Cucumbers, Croutons, Peppers
Cold Patio Paella*
Dried Figs Stuffed with Toasted Almonds
Sangría (see Index)

* Recipe follows

Joan's Gazpacho

Gazpacho is really a type rather than a recipe. And everyone has his preference. This is the best easy Gazpacho I've ever made—using tomato juice eliminates all that mess of chopping and seeding fresh tomatoes (purists, forgive!).

¾ cup diced onion	1½ cups water
¾ cup chopped green pepper	½ cup wine vinegar
¾ cup diced cucumber	4 tablespoons olive oil
2 cloves garlic, minced	Fresh ground pepper
2 cups tomato juice	

Bowls of accompaniments

Croutons	Tomato chunks
Diced cucumber	Chopped green onions

In a blender, combine (in two batches) the onion, green pepper, cucumber, garlic and tomato juice. Blend on high speed until thoroughly mixed. Pour into a bowl and add the water, vinegar, oil and pepper. Chill up to 2 days ahead of time. Serve with the bowls of accompaniments on the table, each person serving himself. Serves 6.

Note: You can make a perfectly good Gazpacho without a blender, dicing the vegetables very, very fine. However, you won't have quite as much bulk and ought to figure on this method serving only 4.

Also, if you're doubling or tripling this recipe for a crowd, go easy on the oil. Use about a third less than the amount doubled or tripled.

Paella Fría
(Cold Paella)

A lovely version for summer or buffet . . . or both. You can cook the chicken and rice the day before and refrigerate separately. (Or cheat by using about one pound of canned chicken.)

1 broiler-fryer, weighing 2½
  to 3 pounds, cut up
1 small onion, peeled and
  sliced
1½ teaspoons salt
Water
1½ cups uncooked long-grain
  rice
2 tablespoons instant minced
  onion
¼ teaspoon crushed saffron
1 envelope French salad
  dressing mix
Vegetable oil
Cider vinegar
½ head romaine, separated
  into leaves

2 cans (7 ounces each)
  minced clams, drained
½ pound salami, cubed
3 medium-size tomatoes,
  diced
1 jar (6 ounces) marinated
  artichoke hearts
1 can or jar (4 ounces)
  pimentos, drained and
  diced
1 package (10 ounces)
  frozen peas, cooked and
  drained
½ cup pitted ripe olives
Beer (optional)

Combine the chicken, onion, salt, and 1 cup water in a
medium-size frying pan; cover. Simmer 45 minutes, or until
the chicken is tender. Remove from broth; cool until easy to
handle, then pull off the skin and take the meat from the
bones; cut into bite-size pieces. Strain the broth into a 4-cup
measure for the next step. (You could cook the chicken and
freeze it, even a few weeks beforehand.)

Combine the rice with the instant onion and saffron in a
large saucepan; add water, or beer, to the chicken broth to
measure amount of the liquid called for on the rice package;
stir into the rice. Cook, following label directions. Place in a
large bowl.

Combine the salad-dressing mix with the oil, vinegar and
water, following the directions on the label. Fold into the rice
mixture. Fold the chicken into the rice mixture. Refrigerate
again at least one hour. Line a large shallow serving dish
with the romaine. Fold the clams, salami, tomatoes, artichoke
hearts and liquid, and pimentos into the rice mixture. Arrange on the bed of romaine. Garnish with peas and olives.
Serves 6 (it's really a salad).

COOL POOL KEBOBBING

(For Brunch, Lunch, Cocktails or Dinner Anytime You Like It)

You may find yourself with a group of swimmers to feed. They're having a sporting time in the pool, lake, off the boat, or on the beach and don't all feel like eating at the same time.

Solution? Kebobbing. Set up a hot barbecue nearby (coals will keep hot about two hours). Set up a buffet table of skewers and all the fixings for one or more of the kebobs below. Whoever feels like it can come assemble his own whenever he likes. A casserole of steamed rice will give a complete menu.

If you want to try kebobbing far away from your kitchen, you might even prepare the skewers ahead of time, freeze the kebobs, and let them defrost on your way to wherever you're going.

About Skewers

I prefer the thinnest metal skewers to either the thick ones (which tear mushrooms apart) or the wooden ones (which may burn). In a pinch, for a picnic, for example, you could use thin twigs. Very short skewers are good for appetizer kebobs. But be careful handling them—you need tongs to avoid burnt fingers.

About the Fire

Besides a barbecue, an hibachi is excellent for most kebobs. For the appetizer kebobs, you can even hollow out a cabbage; insert a can of sterno into the hollow, and light it when ready.

Kebobs From Which to Ad Lib Your Party

For Appetizers:
  Hibachi Beef Appetizers*
  Teeny-Kebobbers*
  Cold Teeny-Kebobbers*
For Main Courses:
  Beef Kebobs*
  Shrimp Kebobs*
  Hawaiian Hot Dog Kebobs*
For Dessert (or Brunch):
  Grilled Fruit Kebobs*

(Also see Breakfast Kebobs, page 56)

Hibachi Beef Appetizers

For the marinating-and-dunking sauce that makes the day, you can either use a cup of store-boughten Teriyaki or make your own Oriental marinade which is sweet and heady.

2 pounds beef tenderloin, cut in ½-inch squares
Oriental Marinade: Make the marinade on page 204, adding ¾ cup brown sugar

Marinate the beef in the Teriyaki sauce or the Oriental Marinade at least 1 hour. Drain off, and save to heat later for a "dunking" sauce. This amount will appetize 10–12 people.

Assemble

Small skewers for each guest
The bowl of marinated beef cubes
A bowl of the heated marinade

To cook: Each guest spears a cube of meat on his skewer and cooks it about 1 minute on each side. Dunk into the sauce and eat.

Note: For a large party once, I precooked the beef cubes by broiling them 2 minutes early in the day; then stuck them on toothpicks all around a large cabbage holding a can of sterno (see page 38). This method allows you to serve a lot of people somewhat easier, since the "cooking" merely consists of waving the beef through the sterno flame until it is heated.

Teeny-Kebobbers, Hot and Cold

Hot Teeny-Kebobbers:

Small skewers and bowls full of various appetite-whetters can make conversation and give you the fun of ad-libbing whatever appetizers you like. Include a bowl of melted butter and/or barbecue sauce plus a pastry brush to brush the teeny-kebobbers with before cooking. Make any combinations you like from these:

½-inch squares of raw sirloin	Olives (pitted)
Salami chunks	Green pepper squares
Hot dog chunks	Cocktail onions
Ham chunks	Pineapple chunks
Cheese chunks	

Cold Teeny-Kebobbers (instead of or in addition to):

In Spain and South America, colorful cold combinations of tidbits on toothpicks are served called *banderillas*. Use the long cocktail toothpicks. Anything you can thread on a pick can be used, combined as you like.

Pickled vegetables, such as onion, cauliflower, carrot chunks	Ham, salami, sausages or cold meats
Smoked fish	Pitted olives
Anchovies	Shrimp, mussels, clams
Cheese chunks	Pimento

Beef Kebobs

3 pounds beef, cut in 1-inch
    cubes

Marinade:

1 cup olive or salad oil
¼ cup lemon juice or vinegar
1 tablespoon soy sauce
1 teaspoon salt

¼ teaspoon black pepper
¼ teaspoon thyme
Stuffed olives, sliced

For Skewers:

Cherry tomatoes
Green peppers, quartered
Mushrooms

Zucchini, sliced
Onions, in chunks

Combine ingredients for marinade. Pour over beef and let stand overnight. Drain the beef, saving the marinade. Grill with cherry tomatoes, green peppers, mushrooms, zucchini (sliced) and onions (in chunks).

Assemble

Long thin skewers
The bowl of meat
Bowls of each vegetable

A bowl of the marinade and a
pastry brush

To cook: Each guest assembles his own skewer. Brush with marinade. Cook over hot coals, turning occasionally about 15–20 minutes, or until meat is done to taste, basting from time to time. If you prefer the vegetables less well done, thread them on a separate skewer and start them 10 minutes after the meat. Serve with steamed rice or barbecued rice (page 215) if desired. Serves 6.

Shrimp Kebobs

3 pounds jumbo shrimp,
    shelled and deveined
6 slices bacon, cut in squares

2 cans (5 oz. each) water
    chestnuts, sliced

Oriental Marinade:

1 cup dry sherry or sake
⅔ cup soy sauce
⅔ cup olive oil
½ teaspoon ginger

2 cloves garlic, crushed
1 teaspoon minced parsley
    (flakes or fresh)

Try to buy the jumbo Mexican shrimp that run about 10 to

the pound. Shell, devein and marinate them for 30 minutes. (If you like a stronger Oriental flavor, you can marinate longer, but after an hour I think the shrimp get lost.)

Assemble

Long skewers
The bowl of shrimp, drained
 (Save the marinade)
A plate of raw bacon
 squares

A bowl of sliced water
 chestnuts
A bowl of the marinade,
 heated

To cook: Each person threads his skewer with the shrimp, raw bacon and water chestnuts; then broils it over hot coals about 12 minutes. Serve with steamed or barbecued rice (page 215) and slices of fresh tomatoes. Use the heated marinade as a sauce. Serves 6.

Note: If your skewers are too thick and the water chestnuts fall off (which mine have done), don't despair. Heat them with the marinade and serve separately.

Hawaiian Hot Dog Kebobs

Assemble

8 hot dogs, cut into 5 chunks
 each
2 cans (10½ ounces each)
 pineapple chunks in a
 bowl

8 teaspoons vegetable oil
 and a pastry brush
8 hot dog rolls, warmed
Barbecue sauce (about
 ¾ cup)

To cook: On a skewer, alternate hot dog chunks with pineapple chunks. Brush with vegetable oil. Broil over hot coals, turning until browned. Meanwhile, spread each roll with barbecue sauce. Slide hot dogs off skewers and onto the rolls. Makes 8 servings of 1 hot dog each.

Grilled Fruit Kebobs

12 large, firm strawberries,
 hulled
12 pitted dates
3 ripe, firm peaches, peeled
 and quartered

3 ripe, firm unpeeled
 bananas, cut into 2-inch
 chunks

Basting Sauce

⅓ cup Port wine
2 tablespoons honey
2 tablespoons melted butter
2 tablespoons orange juice
1 teaspoon cornstarch

½ teaspoon grated orange rind
¼ teaspoon dry mustard
⅛ teaspoon cinnamon
⅛ teaspoon ginger

Mix the cornstarch with orange juice. Make sauce by combining Port, honey, melted butter, the orange juice with cornstarch, orange rind, mustard, cinnamon and ginger in a small saucepan. Cook slowly, stirring constantly, until thickened and clear; keep warm.

Assemble

Thin skewers
Bowls full of the fruits

The bowl of hot basting sauce and a pastry brush

To cook: Each guest arranges his own fruit on a skewer, alternating colors and shapes and peeling the banana chunks. He then brushes hot sauce over the fruit kebob and grills it over hot coals about 10 minutes, turning occasionally and brushing with additional sauce. Serves 6.

REAL NICE CLAMBAKES

for beach—barbecue—or stove

Those who love steamers need no hard-sell on the glories of a piled-high bowl of hot clams, mugs of steamy broth, melted lemon butter and lots of hot French bread for dunking. What you may not know is that you can steam clams practically anywhere, with or without the official two-quart clam steamer.

About Cleaning Clams

No matter where you cook them, the clams should be soaked in a sink-full of cold water, changing the water several times.

Scrub them with a stiff brush under running water, after the final soak.

About Liquid to Steam Clams In

There are dedicated partisans advocating all kinds of liquid for that inch in the bottom of the pan, since it mixes with the clam juice to produce the all-important broth. You can always use plain water, but I prefer white wine or beer. Either the wine or the beer produces a heady, and quite different, broth.

About Serving and Eating Clams

For those new to clamdom, the process goes like this. Skin off the dark covering on the tail of a steamer (cherrystones don't have this). Hold the clam by the tail, dunk it first into the broth and then into butter. Eat it. Sip the broth as you go.

A Sandblast Clambake

Invite your crew to a twilight dinner on the beach (local ordinances permitting). Given a fire pit lined with seaweed, you can steam clams and lobsters and corn.

Dig a hole in the sand, and line it with rocks. Build a kindling fire in the hole to heat the rocks to red hot.

When the rocks are hot, line the hole with a piece of wet canvas. Put a layer of seaweed on top. Lay in the clams and/or lobsters and corn, with silk removed but husks left on. Cover with another layer of seaweed and close tightly with another piece of wet canvas, held down by rocks. It will take 30–35 minutes for the clams to steam.

While the clams steam, you can cool beer by piling cans in a net. Let the net drift in water (be sure to secure one end!).

Stay-Home Clambake

This is a one-pot meal for 4 to 6 very hungry people. In the bottom of a clam steamer: Use 3 pints of liquid (see above). Load the top of the steamer in this order:

A layer of wet seaweed
  (everybody helps you
  pick it at the shore) or
  lettuce leaves
2 broiler chickens, quartered
8 unpeeled medium potatoes,
  regular or sweet
8 unpeeled medium onions

4 ears of corn, silk removed,
  but husks on
4 dozen small clams
  (wrapped in cheesecloth,
  a dozen to a package,
  for easier serving)
4 one-pound live lobsters

Cover the top with more seaweed. In the center put a potato which you test with a fork by and by. When the potato is done, so is the clambake. Steam over a charcoal grill for about 1½ hours. (You can also cook this on top of the stove.)

Note: If you have trouble fitting the lid on, use foil as a cover.

Improvising Clambakes

On the stove or charcoal grill:

If you don't have a clam steamer, use a colander that fits into a saucepan large enough so that all the holes are covered by the pan. Use about an inch of liquid in bottom of saucepan. Put clams in the top section. Steam 15 to 20 minutes, covered, until clams open. For charcoal grill, just be sure the coals are red hot; place container on the grill. Add more coals if need be. The cooking time should be the same. Serve with the broth from the bottom of the pan.

In the oven:

Fill a large roasting pan with liquid to 1 inch. Stir in one tablespoon salt. Add clams (and ears of corn, too, if you like). Cover with a lid or foil. Bake at 350° for 20 to 25 minutes until clams open. Serve with the broth at the bottom of the pan.

Leftover Clam Broth: Heavenly Clam Soup

We first invented this when we were left with a quart of broth after a clambake. It's worth cooking the clams first to get the makings for this. Served icy cold, in mugs, it's heavenly. If you can't wait, use bottled clam juice.

When To Cook?

In the morning, or the day before. The broth, itself, can be frozen until ready to use.

4 cups clam broth cooked with wine or beer or 2 cups bottled clam juice mixed with 1 cup white wine and 1 cup chicken broth	4 cups heavy cream 1 can (6½ ounces or more) minced clams 1 or 2 cucumbers, peeled and finely chopped Salt and pepper to taste

Pour the cream slowly into cold clam broth or the clam juice and white wine mix. Stir in the minced clams, chopped cucumbers, and season to taste. Chill. Serves 8.

SOME REAL FINE BARBECUES

The trouble with most barbecuing is that unless you're doing hamburgers and hot dogs and a fruit bowl for dessert, you never end up doing the entire menu outdoors. Instead, you're running from kitchen to patio checking something, and back in again. Or you're in the kitchen while your husband yells, "Ready!—Where's the blank-blank platter?"

My point here is to give you one basic plan for an entire menu to be cooked over an outdoor grill. There's almost always some kitchen preparation ahead of time, but at least you can count on bringing your drink outside and being where the action is.

Barbecue Recipes From Which to Ad Lib a Menu

Appetizers
    Hot Teeny-Kebobbers (*see Index*)
    Shrimp Kebobs (*See Index. Use smaller shrimp.*)

Main Dishes
    Steak*
    London Broil*
    Barbecued Butterfly Lamb*
    Barbecued Corn Beef*
    Barbecued Spare Ribs*

Accompaniments
    Barbecued Rice*
    Barbecued Vegetables*

Dessert
    Fruit Kebobs (*see Index*)

Steak

There's not much you can do wrong with a steak, except over-cook it. But you might consider enlarging your steak file to include other than beef (liver steaks, lamb steaks, ham steaks, fish steaks, for instance).

And you might want to try different ways of cooking them.

Cooking Steak

The leave-it-alone school says plunk on the meat. No salt. No nothing. Just grill. You can tell when meat is done by pressing it. If it's spongy, it's probably still too rare. As the steak cooks, it becomes hard to the touch. At this point, make a cut near the bone, and see if it's done to your taste.

The marinade school says let the steak soak up the flavor of whatever you're using. Which is also supposed to seal in the juices. Some good marinades follow.

The salt school says cook steak in a thick coating of coarse salt which keeps the outside of a steak from getting charcoaly and crusty. Here's how you do it. You need a steak at least 2½ inches thick (or else the salt will over-flavor the meat). Mix 5 cups of kosher (or any coarse) salt with enough water to make a paste. Spread a layer half an inch thick on each side of the steak. Put a wet paper towel on top of the salt. Grill about 25 minutes *on each side* for rare. (You can test by making a small cut in the center.) Knock off the salt crust and slice.

Marinades and Sauces for Steaks Of All Kinds

Almost anything flavorsome you can dream up can be used as a marinade. You have only to give the marriage of meat and marinade enough time—either overnight in the refrigerator, or at least three hours at room temperature.

I hate to waste all that lovely stuff after the meat is removed for grilling, so, depending on what that lovely stuff is (burnt butter won't do), I either heat up the rest to do double-duty as sauce later, or play with it to make super-sauce. Such as reducing a wine marinade and adding a bit of cream or butter. You can heat the sauce in a pan right on the barbecue.

As for basting, I've never been sure that it makes that much difference (except for fish steaks where it does), and I hate to see all that potential sauce dripping into the fire.

Quick marinades

1. Bottled barbecue sauce
2. Bottled salad dressing
3. Onions in butter (for beef): Brown onions in butter until both the onions and the butter are dark brown. Rub this over steak.
4. Prepared mustard
5. Wine and oil

Marinade Exotica, For Beef

½ cup olive oil
1 large clove garlic, crushed
1 teaspoon salt
½ teaspoon coarsely ground
    black pepper
½ teaspoon dry mustard

1½ tablespoons Roquefort
    cheese
2 teaspoons instant coffee
    (powder)
2 tablespoons dry vermouth

Blend the ingredients to make a thick sauce. Rub into steak. Let stand at room temperature at least 3 hours. This makes enough for a 4-pound beef steak.

Drunken Beef Marinade

9 tablespoons bourbon
    whiskey or red wine
6 tablespoons soy sauce
2 tablespoons garlic vinegar
2 tablespoons oil

½ teaspoon salt or smoked
    salt
½ teaspoon almost any herb
½ teaspoon freshly ground
    pepper

Combine all ingredients and mix well. Pour over meat. Cover. Drain meat when ready to broil. For 4 to 6 pounds of beef.

Pacific Marinade for Swordfish or Lamb Steaks

1 cup honey
½ cup soy sauce
¼ cup lemon juice

Salt, pepper and garlic to
    taste

Combine ingredients. Pour over. For swordfish, save most of the marinade to heat as sauce. Use a little to baste with while cooking. For 2–3 pounds fish or meat.

London Broil

2 pounds flank steak
1 cup Wishbone Italian
    Dressing
6 tablespoons lime juice

1 tablespoon coarse salt
Pepper
Sliced onion rings

Score the steak in diagonal cuts. Mix the dressing with the lime juice and seasonings. Pour over meat. Lay the sliced onions around meat. Marinate at room temperature at least 3 hours. Broil over coals, or in the oven.

Barbecued Butterfly Lamb

7 to 8 pound leg of lamb (Ask your butcher to bone it and butterfly it. Then ask him to flatten the two "wings" with a cleaver, to get the lamb into a fairly even steak).

Coarse salt

Marinade:

1 cup salad oil
⅓ cup wine vinegar
2 to 3 cloves garlic, crushed
Ground black pepper

2 tablespoons fresh dill, or 1 tablespoon dried dillweed

Sprinkle salt generously over the lamb. Mix all the other ingredients into a marinade and pour over. Turn the lamb now and again if you remember. Marinate at least 3 hours.

Cook for 45 minutes over hot coals. Baste occasionally. Watch out for flames as the oil drips. Don't overcook. This is delicious on the pink side. Serve sliced diagonally as you would beefsteak. Serves 6–8.

Barbecued Corn Beef

There's a lot of water-throwing in the preparations, but it's worth it. This is a wonderful change from the usual barbecue. Serve with hot rye bread, or in warm rye rolls put on the grill and warmed in foil about 15 minutes before the corn beef is done.

5 pounds corn beef
3 onions, cut in halves
Pickling spices

3 stalks celery cut in halves
2 cloves of garlic

To cook ahead: Cover corn beef with water and cook until it boils. Throw off water. Cover corn beef with water again and cook until it boils. Throw off water again. Cover corn beef with water, add onions, pickling spices, garlic and celery and simmer 3 hours. Cool. Score corn beef and dot with cloves. Refrigerate up to 2 days.

Sauce
½ cup brown sugar   2 tablespoons mustard
½ cup catsup

About 45 minutes before serving: Combine sauce ingredients. Spread sauce over corn beef. Barbecue on a grill over hot coals, 15 minutes on one side, 15 minutes on the other. Serves 8.

Barbecued Spareribs in Beer (for Oven or Barbecue)

If you can remember to marinate the ribs overnight in the refrigerator, this is a fine dish to precook early the next morning, go away, and finish up at dinner time, indoors or out.

6 pounds spareribs cut into
    individual portions

Marinade:
3 cups beer   2½ teaspoons dry mustard
1 cup honey   2 teaspoons ginger
2 teaspoons lemon juice   2 teaspoons nutmeg

Combine the ingredients for the marinade in a large bowl. Add the spareribs and marinate either overnight in the refrigerator or three hours at room temperature. Remove the ribs from the marinade, saving the marinade to baste with later. Roast the spareribs 45 minutes in a 425° oven. Drain off the fat. At this point, you can put the ribs aside until later or continue cooking as follows:

For oven: Pour the marinade over the ribs. Roast another 45 minutes at 350°.

For barbecue: Grill the ribs over hot coals with the grill as far away from the fire as possible. Baste frequently with the reserved marinade, turning the ribs as they brown. Grill until tender, about 30 minutes. Serves 6.

Barbecued Rice

You can barbecue or beach-fire-picnic and cook your rice from scratch in aluminum foil pouches. Each pouch will make 4 servings:

1⅓ cups minute rice	Dash Tabasco sauce
1⅓ cups water	Pepper
2 tablespoons minced onion	2 fourteen-inch squares of
½ teaspoon salt	aluminum foil
1 teaspoon prepared mustard	Butter
2 tablespoons chili sauce	

Mix the water with onion, salt, mustard, chili sauce, Tabasco, and pepper. To make the pouch, place the two sheets of foil on top of each other in a bowl. Press into the bowl to form the pouch. Put the rice in the bottom of the pouch. Pour over the seasonings. Dot with butter and seal tightly. Cook over hot coals for 15 minutes. Open the foil and fluff the rice with a fork. For more rice, it's important to make more pouches, as a large amount will not cook properly all in one.

Barbecued Vegetables

Providing your grill is large enough, you can cook your vegetables right along with the meat in a variety of ways.

In a Pan: Whatever you would do on a stove you can do on a pan over the grill—fried onions, sautéed mushrooms, peppers and onions, and so forth.

In Foil Pouches: Double-fold squares of aluminum foil to hold the individual portions of vegetables. Dot with lots of butter, salt and pepper and seal loosely.

(I like to parboil green beans, carrots, pearl onions until they are not-quite-but-almost done. Then I finish them up in foil on the grill, which takes another ten minutes.)

Potatoes: Use slices of white or sweet potatoes. Try ⅛-inch slices of white potatoes and onions. Season with salt, pepper and chopped parsley. Dot with butter. Time: About 20 minutes.

Whole baked white or sweet potatoes will take 45 minutes to 1 hour.

Corn: Husk the corn. Spread with butter, then salt and double-wrap. Time: 10 to 12 minutes.

In the Fire: Potatoes, wrapped in foil, bake wonderfully right in the coals. Small eggplants and whole peppers can be cooked right in the coals, too. Turn them from time to time until tender. Peel back the skins. Eat sprinkled with olive oil, salt and pepper—Spanish-style.

9

FILLING THE GENERATION GAP, Or Why Are Their Mouths Always Open?

Including "Stuff Kids Can Cook for Themselves"
by Alan Jay Reinach, Age 12

"Oh, my friends, be warned by me
That breakfast, dinner, lunch, and tea
Are all the human frame requires.
With that the wretched child expires."

"Henry King"
by Hillaire Belloc

Then there are times the population explosion seems to be taking place only in your house. Your *vacation* house where leisure and pleasure are supposed to be the order of the day.

Whether you have your own darlings raiding the icebox, or grandchildren for a visit, or friends who never go anywhere without the children . . . feeding the kids should certainly be numbered among the facts of second house life.

Which brings me to a small lecture on the number of *no-good* starchy and prepared products on the market we buy for kids because (a) we need snacks around to fill the gap between meals, or (b) the printing on the package looks nice.

If you read the fine print on the labels, you'll become aware of such hydrogenated muck and additives, you hopefully may want to question the wisdom of including those products in your kids' cultural heritage. (Or your own.) End of lecture.

Situation: Snacks

Small boxes of raisins
Dried fruit of any kind—prunes, apricots, figs
Fresh fruit
Vegetables—such as carrot sticks, celery sticks
Cheese and crackers
Cookies (home-made or from the bakery. Check the labels on store-boughten cookies, please?)
Ice Cream—popsicles, Good-humors, etc.
Nuts
Luncheon meats

Situation: Drinks

Besides being always hungry, kids seem to be always thirsty. Colas and carbonated beverages have always been last on my list, though I don't feel so extreme about them as to eliminate them entirely. Better choices would be:

Milk
Chocolate milk
Fruit juices—pineapple, grape, tomato (kids don't seem to go for the tarter juices such as grapefruit)
Lemonade

A good way to get through any one day without whines and carrying-on (or more work for you) is to put a gay pitcher of anything into the refrigerator after breakfast. Put a stack of paper cups nearby. That's "the drink of the day."

Try the same idea if children come to visit. Instead of asking them what they want, bring out a pitcher of something and announce that's what you have. (Then, if a drink is vocally unacceptable, you could offer a substitute.)

Situation: Feeding the Kids First

You may run into two kinds of child-stuffing problems. Either you're having guests for dinner and want to eat late, leisurely, and childless. Or you're invited out and you still have to feed them along with taking a bath, resting, dressing, and so forth.

Solutions

1. If you're cooking a casserole, take some out early. Or take some out before adding wine or all the good things children for some reason find bad.
2. Heat up more of something you cooked yesterday. Plan ahead if you know you're having company or going out. Cook a roast, more of chops you might be having, an extra chicken. Wrap a portion in foil and reheat in a slow oven.
3. Keep small portions of cooked meats in the freezer, ready for situations like this.
4. Cook something quickly such as:
   Cube steaks—frozen French fried potatoes
   Lettuce with bottled salad dressing

Cake (from the freezer)
Milk
> OR

Hamburger sandwiches
Raw carrot and celery sticks
Potato chips
Ice cream (from freezer)
Milk
> OR

Frozen pizza
Salad
Fruit
Milk and cookies

5. Heat TV dinners while you're getting dressed. They are perfectly wonderful solutions for your having an unfrazzled evening. And isn't an unfrazzled Mommy more important than one good meal, more or less?
6. Have your husband take the kids out for a bite.
7. Get the children invited elsewhere.
8. If the kids are old enough, let them cook for themselves. (See recipes following) Give them their own little hibachi away from the kitchen . . . and you.

Situation: A Child-Centered Dinner (That You'll Like, Too)

This is a menu you might enjoy for a birthday party, or a dinner where the children outnumber the grownups.

Tomato Juice Cocktails (Kids love Bloody Marys before the vodka goes in. Do a pitcher for them, and a pitcher of the stronger stuff for you . . . see Index.)
Steak Roll-Ups*
Corn on the Cob
Raw Vegetable Platter
Doughnut Sandwiches*
Beverages

Steak Roll-Ups

Cube steaks, 3½×5 inches
Seasoned tenderizer
Stick of Cheddar cheese
  (1 for each steak)

Dill pickles (1 slice for each
  steak)
Butter

Moisten both sides of the cube steaks with water and sprinkle on seasoned tenderizer. Place a stick of Cheddar cheese and a dill pickle on each steak. Roll up and fasten with metal skewers. Grill, brushing occasionally with butter. (Either in oven or over charcoal grill.)

Doughnut Sandwiches

4 cake doughnuts
1 milk chocolate candy bar,
  sliced into fourths

4 large marshmallows, sliced
  in half

This takes about 10 minutes, just before you eat.

Slice the doughnuts in half, lengthwise. Lay pieces of candy on 4 of the halves. Lay 2 marshmallow halves on the other 4 halves.

Heat in a pan (over stove, campfire, barbecue) until the chocolate and the marshmallows begin to melt. Make "sandwiches" by putting together a chocolate and a marshmallow half. Serves 4.

Situation: Home from Camp Cookout

You can handle any number of hungry-for-home-cooking kids (which I think means *your* hamburgers as opposed to *their* hamburgers) and parents with this cookout.

Barbecued Hamburgers and Hot Dogs* or Frankburgers*
Warm Buns
Bowls of Accompaniments: Onion Rings, Relish, Mustard, Celery
  and Carrot Sticks, Cole Slaw, Potato Chips, Catsup
Make Your Own Sundaes*
Milk—Soft Drinks—Beer (for parents)

HAMBURGERS AND HOT DOGS

I've long suspected that hamburgers and hot dogs, not Wall Street, are what keeps the economy going. So the information assembled here assumes you already have some favorite styles. Hamburger seasoning, particularly, like the stock market, depends on the weather and your mood. (And in the case of onions, who's the dominant personality in your family.)

About hamburgers and hot dogs in general:

1. Beef ground just once makes the steakiest hamburgers. (If your supermarket butcher complains, tell him you want to eat it raw and you're afraid if it's already packaged.)
2. Stick an ice chip and a small piece of butter into the middle of a hamburger patty before broiling. The meat will stay especially moist.
3. Hot dogs taste better grilled or pan fried.
4. Any bun for hamburgers or hot dogs tastes better wrapped in foil and warmed. You might also try individual hero buns for either.
5. Use hot dog buns for hamburgers and vice-versa. Shape hamburgers into sausage shapes. Cut hot dogs to fit buns. This is a good idea when you have more of one than the other.

Cooking Hamburgers For A Crowd

One of the problems of cooking a lot of hamburgers is that the cook has to stand over the grill, watching and waiting. Here's a method to do ahead that can get a lot of hamburgers ready at one time.

Panfry hamburger patties in butter, very rare; or barbecue.

Split and butter hamburger buns. Lay a patty in each bun (adding anything you'd like, see below). Wrap each sandwich loosely in foil, sealing the edges well. You can do all this ahead of time.

When ready to serve: heat in a 300° F. oven for 15 minutes. If your group still isn't ready, turn off the oven. The hamburgers will keep fine for 30–45 minutes.

Toppings For Hamburgers And Hot Dogs

1. Mexican fried beans, a slice of avocado and a sprinkling of chopped chives.
2. Chili
3. Cheeseburgers—besides American cheese, try chive, cream cheese, blue cheese. Scoop out insides of a hero roll and fill with grated Swiss.
4. Sauerkraut
5. Russian: Sauté 2 tablespoons minced onions with a 3 ounce can of sliced mushrooms. Add 1 cup sour cream, ¼ teaspoon Tabasco sauce, 1 tablespoon ketchup and salt to taste. Enough for 8 servings.

Frankburgers

1 cup steak flavor ketchup
1 tablespoon lemon juice
1 teaspoon seasoned salt
¼ teaspoon onion flakes
1 pound ground beef
1 cup soft bread crumbs
 (2 slices)

2 teaspoons parsley flakes
6 frankfurters
6 frankfurter rolls
½ cup sliced green onions

Blend ketchup, lemon juice, seasoned salt, and onion in a 1 cup measure.

Combine ground beef, bread crumbs, parsley flakes, and ½ cup of the ketchup mixture in a large bowl; mix lightly until well blended. Divide into 6 even mounds.

Pat each mound into a rectangle, 6"×4", on a sheet of waxed paper; top with a frankfurter. Roll up tightly, jelly-roll fashion, using waxed paper as a guide; pinch edges to seal. Brush with part of the remaining ketchup mixture; place on grill about 6 inches above hot coals.

Grill, turning several times and brushing with remaining ketchup mixture, 10 minutes, or until beef is as done as you like it.

While meat cooks, toast rolls on side of grill; butter, if you wish. Place each meat roll in a frankfurter roll; sprinkle it with green onions. Serves 6.

MAKE YOUR OWN SUNDAES

Depending on how many people you have, you can make ice cream balls early in the day, pile them in a bowl and freeze them. Serve from an ice bucket. Or just bring the ice cream cartons right to the buffet table and scoop as you go. We've never had trouble with the ice cream melting (it goes too fast), but you could stand the cartons in pans of ice.

Ice cream—at least three different flavors

Toppings: (1 cup will make 6 sundaes)
A bowl of hot fudge sauce, kept warm over a candle warmer
Or cold chocolate sauce
A bowl of strawberry sauce
A bowl of butterscotch sauce
A bowl of marshmallow sauce
Sliced bananas. Other sliced fruits, if desired
A bowl of red and green maraschino cherries
A bowl of chopped nuts
Whipped cream, in a bowl
Paper dessert bowls
Wooden spoons
Ice cream spoons

About the toppings:

You can buy almost any topping you want. Or make them yourself.

Hot Fudge Sundae Sauce

½ pound (two 4 ounce bars)   ¼ cup brandy, rum, or
   sweet cooking chocolate   kirsch (or cream for the
½ cup strong black coffee   children)

Melt the chocolate and coffee together in the top of a double boiler until the sauce is very smooth. Stir in the brandy. Makes 1 cup.

Butterscotch Sauce

½ cup brown sugar   ½ teaspoon salt
½ cup light corn syrup   2 tablespoons butter
½ cup cream   1 teaspoon vanilla

In the top of a double boiler, over low heat, mix the sugar, corn syrup and cream. Cook 30 minutes, stirring occasionally. Add the rest of the ingredients. Good hot or cold.

MAKE-YOUR-OWN-SANDWICH BUFFET

Situation: Teenagers Without Trauma

Whatever you would cook they wouldn't like anyway, so this menu where they make their own everything eliminates *that* game!

Set up everything on the porch, or down by the lake . . . anywhere outdoors. Get a pair of ear-plugs for yourself, and relax.

*Make-Your-Own-Sandwich Buffet**
Potato Chips
Potato Salad
Olives (pitted)
Bottles and Cans of Soft Drinks in a Tub of Ice
Ice Cream Sandwiches (brought down from your freezer later)
    or
All Kinds of Cookies and Grapes (seedless)
    (Try to avoid anything with pits which you may be stumbling over for weeks to come.)

This isn't the cheapest way to handle a crowd of teenagers, but it's easy! You buy everything. And it works for us grownups too as a lunch; a casual party. The secret is in the style—to arrange everything nicely, in baskets, on boards; perhaps dill pickles in flower pots—so your table has some character and it doesn't look as though you're eating in Louie's Delicatessen.

Here's a map for one sandwich buffet, but substitute any meats and breads you like.

On platters:

Sliced tongue or ham	Slices of Swiss cheese
Sliced turkey	Sliced tomatoes
Sliced corn beef and/or pastrami	Cooked crisp bacon (optional)

In bowls:

Shredded lettuce	Mustard
Chopped liver	Ketchup
Cole slaw	Mayonnaise
Russian dressing	

In baskets:

Rye bread, sliced	Hard and soft rolls, split
Egg bread, sliced	and buttered

Each guest builds his own sandwich—as fanciful as he

likes—such as turkey, chopped liver and bacon. Or corn beef, cole slaw and tomatoes.

A NOTE TO THE TEACHER

My son, Alan, has generously consented to share some of his cook's secrets in the next few pages. All of which are good, I think, allowing for the fact that his food gets devoured by him and I usually get the job of vacuuming the kitchen.

It's a good idea to get your children involved in cooking—and a second house is a great place to learn. There's more time and usually more nothing-to-do days. That's about all I want to add to Alan's careful analysis except for a few pointers you may care to pass on to your children:

1. Please take out the fried bologna before the pan turns black.
2. Please put cold water in the blender after you make thick shakes. Do not take the blender into your room for more than two days!
3. Please do not walk in the cinnamon with bare feet.
4. Please do not eat all the brownie batter before baking.

STUFF KIDS* CAN COOK FOR THEMSELVES

by
Alan Jay Reinach, age 12

Introduction

Many parents think that their kids should not be taught to cook. Or that it's not necessary for them to learn. Or maybe it doesn't occur to them.

* Kids: Anybody who's tall enough to reach the counters and stove is tall enough to cook.

But, girls especially should be able to cook because, when they are married, it will come in handy.

Boys are seldom taught to cook. After all, why would boys need to cook? But, boys especially should be able to cook because, when *they* are married, it will come in handy. (After all, a fella never knows if his wife-to-be can cook.)

And when kids are left alone at home, or no one will cook for them, and they're hungry, cooking ability is good to have.

Things To Remember

1. You should always wash your hands before cooking.
2. Take out everything you're gonna need before you start.
3. Read the recipe first and make sure you have the time and the ingredients to make it.
4. Make sure you like what you're making.
5. Remember to put away all your ingredients when you are done.
6. Remember to clean the dirty dishes you used or put them by the sink for your mother to clean up if she's dumb enough to do it for you.

Easy-to-Prepare Packaged Foods

There are a lot of things you can make simply by following the instructions on the back of the package.

1. Frozen pizzas
2. TV dinners
3. Gelatin desserts
4. Cookie mixes
5. Canned and packaged soups
6. Jiffy popcorn (the kind that comes ready to pop in its own container)
7. Quick thaw frozen fruits
8. Frozen juices

Easy-to-Cook Stuff

Ketchupburgers

1 pound hamburger meat	Otherwise use frozen
¾ cup ketchup or barbecue	minced onions or dried
sauce	onion flakes, Mom)
1 medium onion, chopped	Salt
(for kids over 10.	

Put the hamburger meat in a bowl. Add about half of your measure of ketchup, the chopped onion and salt to taste. Use your hands to mix everything together.

You can make good patties by grabbing a chunk of meat, rolling it into a ball, and squishing it down until it looks like a fat pancake. Make all the patties.

Put a little cooking oil in a large frying pan. Heat until the oil is hot. Put in the patties and let them brown quickly on both sides (use a spatula to turn them with).

Then spread a little of the rest of the ketchup on top of each hamburger. Turn the hamburgers over, and spread the bottoms with ketchup. Let them cook until they're done the way you like them. This will make 4–6 patties.

Super Heros

Slice a small hero bread the long way. Spread butter, mustard, and mayonnaise on each half. On one half, place a thin layer of lettuce. Add some sliced onion. Make a layer of American cheese. Add a layer of bologna, and 2 slices of ham. Add another slice of bologna and another slice of cheese. Top it off with more lettuce and onion. Put the other half of the bread on top.

Now doesn't that sound good?

Tuna à la Cheese (for 4)

Pour the oil out of a can of tuna fish. Put the tuna fish in a bowl and mix evenly with about a tablespoon of mayonnaise (more if you like more), 3 chopped pickle chips (say it fast three times), and some onion salt to taste. Put in some chopped celery if you have it.

Spread the tuna fish evenly on four slices of white bread. Top each with a slice of American cheese. Put the sandwiches in a pan or on a cookie sheet. Heat under the broiler until the cheese is melted like it is in a cheeseburger.

Deviled Eggs

2 eggs
2 teaspoons mayonnaise
Pinch of chopped parsley

A couple of pinches of paprika

Boil the eggs for 15 minutes starting with cold water. Start counting from the time the water starts to boil and turn down your fire then, so the eggs don't boil too hard.

When the eggs are done, put them under cold water and remove the shells without breaking the egg. I mean, just peel around the egg.

Slice each egg into half, the long way. Take out the yolks and put them in a little bowl. Add mayonnaise and parsley to the yolks. Mash together with a fork till everything is mixed evenly.

With a spoon, fill the empty egg whites with the yolk mixture, keeping the halves separate. Sprinkle paprika on top of each stuffed egg and serve. Serves 1 hearty appetite.

Extra Thick Thick Shakes

4 medium scoops of ice
  cream (any flavor)
1 cup milk
2 teaspoons malted milk
  powder

2 tablespoons chocolate
  syrup

Put all the ingredients into a blender. Be sure the top is on. The secret is to blend it very quickly, no more than 10 seconds so it will be thick. Serves 1 extra-large appetite.

Cinnamon Toast

2 pieces of white bread   1 teaspoon sugar
1 teaspoon cinnamon   Butter

First, mix the cinnamon and sugar together.

Then toast the bread to your liking. And butter it. Then sprinkle the sugar and cinnamon mix evenly over the toast. For 1.

Note: This is also tasty with raisin bread.

Ham and Eggs

1 sliced cooked ham   Butter or margarine
2 eggs   Salt

Chop the ham into small pieces. Put the eggs in a bowl and beat well. Add salt to the eggs.

Melt the butter in a small frying pan. Put the ham in and cook it until slightly brown. Pour the egg mixture over. Use a fork to stir the eggs until they are cooked to your taste. For 1.

Note: This recipe can also be made using potatoes, bacon, onions, steak and other things in place of the ham.

Frozen Fruit

1 can fruit cocktail   Whipped cream in a spray
                               can

Stick the can of fruit in the freezer, or in the ice cube section of the refrigerator. After 3 hours or so, bring it out and let it stand for 5 minutes. Open both ends and push out the frozen fruit. Slice into rounds. Spray whipped cream on top. Will serve 1 person 4 times (if you keep putting it back in the freezer), or 4 people once.

Very Good Brownies

These are good because they taste good and it only takes one pan to mix the stuff in.

4 squares bitter chocolate
½ cup shortening (you can use 1 stick of butter, or half a stick of butter, and ¼ cup of Crisco)
1½ — 1¾ cups sugar

4 eggs
1 cup flour, sifted, or use the already sifted kind
½ teaspoon salt
1 cup chopped walnuts (optional)

Put the chocolate and the butter in a large saucepan. Turn the fire on very low and heat the chocolate and butter just until they melt together.

Add in everything else in order. Stir well each time you add something.

Grease a square pan. Heat the oven to 350° F.

Spread the batter in the pan. Bake for 30 minutes. Let them cool. The first day they will be like cake. The second day they will get more fudge-y. *large pan 24 min.*

Fried Bologna

Dear Bologna Lovers:

You are not to be forgotten. Here is a recipe that will suit your bologna taste. All you do is put the bologna into a pan and cook until brown, turning occasionally. No butter needed.

Your fellow Bologna lover,

Alan Reinach

Appendix

STORING AND FREEZING
(Leftovers too)
and AN OPENING THE HOUSE CHECKLIST

Note: The freezer times given, following, are less than those generally recommended by the United States Department of Agriculture and other home economics groups. This is because it's my opinion that the freezer functions best for short-term storage; the sooner the frozen food is used, the better its taste seems to be.

Breads, Cakes and Cereals

Store in original wrapper in breadbox or refrigerator. Bread stays fresh longer at room temperature than when chilled, but in hot, humid weather, refrigeration protects it better against mold.

FREEZER: Breads and cakes are indispensable freezer items for vacation houses; be sure you buy replacements as needed.

LEFTOVER: Whirl in blender, and use in the 100 ways you use breadcrumbs—on *gratinées*, over stewed tomatoes, as breading for chops and chicken, etc.

CEREALS, FLOURS, SPICES AND SUGAR: Store at room temperatures in tightly closed containers that keep out dust, moisture, and insects. During the summer, buy in small quantities. Inspect for weevils. Leftover cereals can be crisped in very slow oven.

DRY MIXES (CAKE, PANCAKE, MUFFIN, ROLL, ETC.) To protect from insects, transfer contents to glass jar. Cut out recipe panel and paste on jar so you know what it is and how to use. Store in pantry at room temperature.

Cocktail Tidbits, Nuts, Honey and Sirups

Leftover jars of water chestnuts, or similar cocktail treats, crackers, potato chips, fried noodles, etc.—all can be frozen and used the following week. Warm the crackers, chips, etc. in a slow oven to restore freshness. Save the juice from pickle jars, pickled artichokes, etc.; you can use it to marinate blanched vegetables such as green beans and carrots, and convert them into your own cocktail vegetables.

HONEY AND SIRUPS: Store at room temperature until opened. After their containers are opened, honey and sirups are better protected from mold in the refrigerator. If crystals form, dissolve them by placing container of honey or sirup in hot water.

NUTS: Store in airtight containers in the refrigerator. Because of their high fat content, nuts require refrigeration to delay development of rancidity. Unshelled nuts keep better than shelled. Unsalted nuts keep better than salted because salt speeds rancidity.

Blanched and/or toasted nuts can be frozen in plastic bags and used as needed (for baking, etc.). Freeze opened cans of nuts in original containers, thaw, and warm in very slow oven to restore crispness.

PEANUT BUTTER: Refrigerate open jar. Remove it from the refrigerator a short time before using to allow it to soften for sandwich spread.

Eggs

Store promptly in refrigerator. To insure best quality and flavor, use within a week. If eggs are held too long, the thick white may thin, the yolk membrane may weaken and break when shell is opened.

FREEZER: Grate hard-cooked yolks and freeze in small dishes or ice cube trays; package in bags. Defrost and use as garnish for open sandwiches, vegetables, salads.

Pack raw egg whites in small containers. Then thaw and beat as necessary for recipe.

LEFTOVER: Cover leftover yolks with cold water; refrigerate them, as well as extra egg whites, in a covered container. Use leftover yolks and whites within a week or two in scrambled eggs, sauces, added to cake or roll mixes.

Fats and Oils

Most fats and oils need protection from air, heat, and light. Fats and oils in partially-filled containers keep longer if they are transferred to smaller containers in which there is little or no air space.

BUTTER, FAT DRIPPINGS, AND MARGARINE: Store, tightly wrapped or covered, in refrigerator. Use within 2 weeks. Keep only as much butter or margarine in the butter compartment of the refrigerator as you need for immediate use. Don't let butter or margarine stand for long periods at room temperature; exposure to heat and light hastens rancidity.

FREEZER: Butter can be frozen in original wrappings and will hold for months. Will thaw in about an hour.

BUTTER BALLS FOR COMPANY: Scoop out from large brick of butter using small melon ball scoop or butter paddle. Freeze on flat surface or in ice cube tray. Will thaw in 15–20 minutes.

COOKING AND SALAD OILS: Keep small quantities at room temperature and use before flavor changes. For long storage, refrigerate. Some oils may cloud and solidify in the refrigerator. This is not harmful. If warmed to room temperature, they will become clear and liquid.

HYDROGENATED SHORTENINGS AND LARD: Most firm vegetable shortenings and lard have been stabilized by hydrogenation or antioxidants. Cover and hold at room temperature without damage to flavor.

MAYONNAISE AND OTHER SALAD DRESSINGS: Bought mayonnaise and other salad dressings should be refrigerated after jars have been opened.

Leftover bacon fat can be poured off into a tin container partially filled with water. (Use an old coffee can.) The clean fat will rise to the top and solidify. Scoop it out and transfer to a storage jar. Refrigerate. Use particularly for deep-fat frying and fried chicken.

Fruits

Plan to use fresh fruits promptly while they are sound and at their best flavor. Because fruits are fragile they need special handling to keep them from being crushed or bruised. The softened tissues of bruised or crushed fruits permit the entrance of spoilage organisms that quickly break down quality. Sort fruits before storing. Discard bruised or decayed fruit to keep it from contaminating sound, firm fruit.

Leftover fruits, canned or frozen, can be cut up and served with cream or breakfast cereal or used on ice cream as dessert.

APPLES: Store uncovered in the refrigerator. Unripe or hard apples are best held at cool room temperature (60° to 70°) until ready to eat. Use ripe apples within a week.

APRICOTS, AVOCADOS, GRAPES, NECTARINES, PEARS, PEACHES, PLUMS, AND RHUBARB: When these fruits are ripe, store uncovered in the refrigerator. Use within 3 to 5 days. When unripe, allow to ripen in the open air at room temperature. Do not place in the sun.

BANANAS: Store at room temperature; use when fully ripe.

BERRIES AND CHERRIES: Keep whole, uncovered and unwashed in the refrigerator until ready to use. Washing and stemming these fruits before refrigerating results in loss of food value and increased spoilage. Use within 1 or 2 days. In freezer, they will last for months.

CITRUS FRUITS AND MELONS: These fruits are best stored at a cool room temperature (60° to 70°). But short-time holding in the refrigerator is not harmful to their quality. If citrus fruits are held too long at too-low temperature, the skin becomes pitted and the flesh discolors. Use these fruits within a week.

PINEAPPLES: If fully ripe, these may be refrigerated for a day or two. Wrap them tightly to prevent other foods from taking up the odor of the pineapple. If pineapples are not ripe, keep them above refrigerator temperature.

CANNED FRUITS AND JUICES: After canned fruits and canned fruit juices have been opened, cover, and store in the refrigerator. They can be safely stored in their original containers.

DRIED FRUITS: Keep in tightly closed containers. Store at room temperature, except in warm, humid weather; then, refrigerate.

FROZEN FRUIT JUICES: Cover reconstituted fruit juice concentrates and keep in the refrigerator. For best flavor, keep in glass or plastic containers. Can be stored in freezer for months in their original containers.

LEFTOVER FRUIT JUICES: Use as liquid in making gelatin molds. Boil down to concentrate and add cornstarch to make sweet sauce for glamorizing beets, carrots, squash. Combine 1 part juice with 3 parts mayonnaise and use as salad dressing. Can replace other liquid in breads, muffins, cakes, etc. Use instead of water in "Summer Fruit Bowl" (see Index).

JELLIES, JAMS, AND PRESERVES: After these fruit products have been opened, store them, covered, in the refrigerator.

Fish and Shellfish

Store in coldest part of refrigerator, loosely wrapped. Use within 1–2 days.

FREEZING FISH: Most fish (fillets, steaks, drawn or dressed), can be frozen for several months, but if you can possibly do so, use fresh; whisk right from the pier to your dinner table, and you'll have caught fish at its best.

LEFTOVER FISH AND SHELLFISH: Delicious cold in salad, or bake in shells with cream sauce, or add to beaten eggs and cream and bake for soufflé.

Meat and Poultry

COLD CUTS: Store in the refrigerator. Use within 3 to 5 days. A whole salami will keep 2–3 weeks.

CURED AND SMOKED MEATS: Store ham, frankfurters, bacon, bologna, and smoked sausage in the refrigerator in their original packagings. Uncooked cured pork may store longer than fresh, but the fat will become rancid if held too long. Bacon should be eaten within a week for best quality, a half ham in 3 to 5 days, a whole ham within a week. Ham slices should be wrapped tightly. Use within a few days.

POULTRY, MEAT ROASTS, CHOPS, AND STEAKS: Store in coldest part of refrigerator. Loosen wrappings on fresh meat and poultry. They benefit from some circulation of air in the refrigerator. For poultry, short holding—1 or 2 days—is recommended. If I'm holding poultry more than a day, I wash it inside and out with cut lemon half. Roasts, chops, and steaks may be held 3 to 5 days.

GROUND AND MECHANICALLY TENDERIZED MEATS: Store, loosely wrapped, in coldest part of the refrigerator. Use within 1 or 2 days. Ground meats, such as hamburger and fresh bulk sausage, are more likely to spoil than roasts, chops, or steaks because more of the meat surface has been exposed to contamination from air, from handlers, and from mechanical equipment.

VARIETY MEATS: Variety meats (liver, kidneys, brains, poultry giblets, etc.) Store, loosely wrapped, in the coldest part of refrigerator. Use within 1 or 2 days. Before storing poultry giblets, remove them from the separate bag in which they are often packed, rewrap loosely, and refrigerate. Keep a stockpile of giblets in your freezer and use as basis for soup and stock.

LEFTOVER COOKED MEATS AND MEAT DISHES: Cover or wrap loosely in Saran wrap, refrigerate promptly. Use within 1 or 2 days. Can be cut julienne for salad, scrambled eggs, used in chop suey, sandwiches and salads. (See Chapter 5, "Drop-Ins.")

LEFTOVER STUFFING: Remove leftover stuffing from chicken or turkey, cool immediately, and store separately from the rest of the bird. Use within 1 or 2 days.

LEFTOVER GRAVY AND BROTH: Highly perishable. Cover, store in the refrigerator promptly. Use within 1 or 2 days. Leftover gravy and broth can be frozen in small jars or jam bottles and, when thawed, used to flavor soups, sauces and gravies.

FREEZING UNCOOKED MEATS AND POULTRY: Bacon, sausage, and chopped meat can be frozen for a month or so; steaks, chops and roasts even longer. You'll find it works best to make chopped meat into patties before you freeze; stack the patties with layers of freezer paper or wax paper between each layer, so you can easily remove the number you want. Same with steaks. It's a good idea to freeze all meats in family-size portions.

FREEZING COOKED MEATS AND POULTRY: Soups, stews and casseroles are my all-time favorites to freeze. Whatever the excuse—dinner on the stove and someone's asked us out unexpectedly, or it's rainy and I felt like cooking up a storm, or my "day worker" in the city makes marvelous chicken pies—I tuck a meal-in-one pot into my freezer. I even save leftover ham bones and meat trimmings against the day I feel a soupmaking binge coming on. Now *that's* being carefree: not to have to worry about the wherewithal for making a big pot of soup!

Since I don't like keeping casseroles tied up in the freezer, here's a trick I use: I line the casserole with heavy duty aluminum foil (mold it around the outside first, then fit it inside); pour the cooled soup or stew or whatever into the container (leaving space for expansion during freezing), and cover top with foil. When the food is solidly frozen, I take out the liner with its frozen block, overwrap with foil, label, and return to freezer. At serving time, I slip the contents of the foil package into the casserole or pot, and bake or cook it as necessary.

Milk, Cream, Cheese

FRESH MILK AND CREAM: Store in refrigerator at about 40° F. Milk and cream are best stored only 3 to 5 days, although they have been known to keep a week to 10 days depending on the coldness of your refrigerator and how often it is open. You will simply have to experiment with your own refrigerator, and follow the rule "if in doubt, throw it out!"

FREEZING MILK: Yes, Virginia, you can freeze milk *if* it's *not* in a glass bottle (any kind of paper carton is fine). Thaw in the refrigerator. You will have to agitate it to reconstitute either by shaking hard or putting through a blender. The taste and texture may shift slightly, but it is quite safe.

FREEZING CREAM: Store fresh in its container. Thaw heavy cream in the refrigerator and use for whipping. Light cream may be used, thawed or frozen, for sauces.

FREEZING WHIPPED CREAM: Pile on cookie sheet in mounds and let freeze. Then pack frozen mounds in container. Thaw at room temperature for about 10 minutes. Use as topping on pies, pancakes, ice cream.

DRY MILKS: Keep dry milk—either nonfat or whole—in a tightly closed container. *Nonfat dry milk* will keep in good condition for several months on the cupboard shelf at temperatures of 75° F. or lower. Close the container immediately after using. Dry milk takes up moisture and becomes lumpy if long exposed to air. Lumps make reconstitution difficult.

Dry whole milk is marketed only on a small scale, chiefly for infant feeding. Because of its fat content, it does not keep as well as nonfat dry milk; after the container has been opened, dry whole milk should be stored, tightly covered, in the refrigerator. Refrigerate reconstituted dry milk like fresh fluid milk.

EVAPORATED MILK AND CONDENSED MILK: Store at room temperature until opened, then cover tightly and refrigerate like fresh fluid milk.

CHEESE SPREADS AND CHEESE FOODS: After containers of these foods have been opened, store, covered, in the refrigerator.

HARD CHEESES SUCH AS CHEDDAR, PARMESAN AND SWISS: Keep in the refrigerator. Wrap tightly to keep out air. The original packagings may be used. Stored this way, hard cheeses will keep for several months unless mold develops.

LEFTOVERS: Of Cheddar, or Cheddar type cheeses such as Monterey Jack, Emmentaler, fontina, natural Gruyère, even Parmesan, and certainly Swiss, can be grated or cubed and stored in a covered dish in the freezer to use as needed. Or when you've accumulated about a pint, sprinkle it with 2 tablespoons flour and melt it in a double boiler over low heat (a pottery bowl in a saucepan is a quick double boiler). Cover with a white table wine and a pressed or mashed clove of garlic. Stir often and let cheese melt slowly. If you have some kirschwasser, stir in about 2 tablespoons. Now bring the pottery bowl to table and keep hot over a warmer. Have chunks of toasted French bread, which diners spear on fondue forks and dip into melted cheese. Fun fondue.

SOFT CHEESES SUCH AS COTTAGE, CREAM, CAMEMBERT: Store, tightly covered, in the coldest part of the refrigerator. Use cottage cheese within 3 to 5 days, others within 2 weeks.

Vegetables

The fresher vegetables are when eaten, the better. With only a few exceptions, vegetables keep best in the refrigerator.

Sort vegetables before storing them. Discard any that are bruised, soft, or that show evidence of decay or worm injury. The vegetable crisper in your refrigerator performs better if it is at least two-thirds full. If crisper is less full than this, vegetables will keep better if they are put in plastic bags before going into the crisper.

ASPARAGUS: Discard tough parts of stalks. Store in the refrigerator in crisper or in plastic bag. Use within 1 or 2 days. Cooked asparagus can be refrigerated for several days, added to salad or soup, scrambled with eggs and used with curry or cream sauce. Also, top with grated cheese and breadcrumbs and bake.

BROCCOLI AND BRUSSELS SPROUTS: Clean quickly, drip dry and store in refrigerator in crisper or in plastic bag. Use within 1 or 2 days. Leftover cooked broccoli florets can be sautéed in a few tablespoons hot oil to which you've added lots of mashed garlic.

CABBAGE AND CAULIFLOWER: Store in the refrigerator (heads intact) in crisper or in plastic bags. Use cabbage within 1 or 2 weeks, cauliflower within 3 to 5 days. Slice or separate florets just before cooking. Cooked (but still firm) cauliflower and cabbage can be used as vegetable dippers, cut into soup, or reheated in a few tablespoons hot oil and a tablespoon of minced fresh herbs.

CARROTS, BEETS, AND RADISHES: Remove root tips and tops. Store covered in refrigerator. Use within 1 or 2 weeks. Cooked beets or carrots are nice reheated in a sweet sauce made from melted butter, sugar and orange juice concentrate.

GREEN PEAS AND LIMAS: Leave in pods and store in refrigerator. Use within a day or two.

LETTUCE AND OTHER SALAD GREENS: Wash quickly, dry quickly and whisk into refrigerator crisper (or in plastic bags) to hold down loss of moisture. Use within 1 or 2 days. Use outside leaves as "lining" for peas and green beans which are to be cooked, or canned vegetables which are to be heated; add very little water and steam until vegetables are done.

ONIONS: *Dry onions,* stored at room temperature, or slightly cooler, in loosely woven or open-mesh containers, will keep several months. They sprout and decay at high temperature and in high humidity. Keep *green onions* cold and moist in the refrigerator. Store in plastic bags. Use within 1 or 2 days. Cut onions can be wrapped tightly in Saran wrap and re-frigerated. (Use in water for cooking potatoes or with giblets for stock.)

PEPPERS AND CUCUMBERS: Wash and dry. Store in crisper or in plastic bags in the refrigerator. Use within 3 to 5 days. Slices of peeled cucumbers and peppers can be sautéed in butter and served as a vegetable or garnish.

POTATOES (WHITE): Store in a dark, dry place with good ventilation and a temperature of 45° to 50° F. Light causes greening, which lowers eating quality. High temperatures hasten sprouting and shriveling. If necessary to store at room temperature, use within a week.

SPINACH, KALE, COLLARDS, CHARD, AND BEET, TURNIP AND MUS-TARD GREENS: Wash thoroughly in cold water. Lift these leafy green vegetables out of the water as grit settles to the bot-tom of the pan. Drain. Store in refrigerator in crisper or in plastic bags. Use within 1 or 2 days.

SWEET CORN: Store, unhusked and uncovered, in the refrig-erator. Use within 1 or 2 days (or minutes, if you're lucky!) of picking time.

SWEET POTATOES, HARD-RING SQUASHES, EGGPLANT, AND RUTA-BAGAS: Store at cool room temperature around 60° F. Tem-peratures below 50° may cause chilling injury. These will keep several months at 60° F., but only a week at room tem-perature. Try cooked sweet potatoes in casseroles with sliced apples over which you sprinkle brown sugar or honey and fruit juices. Bake half an hour at 350° or sauté in sugar-butter sirup and serve glazed. Also deep fry. Or whip in blender, add cream, fold into beaten eggs, and bake as soufflé.

TOMATOES: Store ripe tomatoes uncovered in the refrigerator. Keep unripe tomatoes at room temperature away from direct sunlight until they ripen. Cover cut tomatoes with Saran wrap.

FROZEN VEGETABLES: You can buy a wide variety of frozen vegetables, and store them for several months at zero temperature. The shelves in the one-door refrigerator-freezer are for temporary storage, since they do not maintain low temperatures. If you don't need a whole package of vegetables, break or cut it apart and put the unused portion back, rather than thaw and refreeze.

Wine

Opened bottles of white wine will keep 6–7 days in the refrigerator. Opened bottles of red wine, since you're not supposed to chill them, will be good for 3–4 days at room temperature—well, almost as good. A Russian friend has informed us that wine will keep indefinitely if you add a tablespoon of vodka to the bottle. However my recommendation is that you count on 10 days using vodka, and taste to see if you like it. If not, you have a great cooking wine. Fortified wines, such as sherry, port, madeira can be kept in the bar more or less indefinitely.

OPENING THE HOUSE CHECKLIST

BAKING SUPPLIES

. . . Baking powder
. . . Baking soda (I use lots of it, for cleaning, mostly)
. . . Cornstarch (You don't need much; could bring some from home)
. . . Flour (all-purpose)
. . . Pancake mix

BEVERAGES

. . . Cocoa (instant)
. . . Coffee, instant and percolator
. . . Juices—tomato, vegetable, fruit (if you use them)
. . . Milk, fresh
. . . Milk, either evaporated, condensed or powdered
. . . Mix for cocktails; quinine water, soda water, etc.
. . . Soft drinks—colas, ginger ale, etc.
. . . Tea, loose or bags (See "Liquor" for additional beverages you buy separately)

BOTTLED SAUCES AND SALAD DRESSINGS

. . . Barbecue sauce and/or Escoffier Sauce Diable (for delicious quick beef sauce)
. . . Ketchup and/or chili sauce
. . . Mayonnaise
. . . Oil
. . . Bottled salad dressing
. . . Soy sauce
. . . Spaghetti sauce
. . . Tabasco and/or Worcestershire sauce
. . . Teriyaki and/or soy sauce (a good quick marinade)
. . . A good wine vinegar

BREADS

. . . Your favorite bread
. . . Bread crumbs
. . . Crackers (also see page 81)
. . . English muffins

CANNED GOODS

. . . Fruits: 2 to 3 cans of family favorites; also, if space permits, guest specialties like papaya, mandarin oranges, Hawaiian fruit and guava shells
. . . Meat: canned chicken and/or a canned ham; tuna fish; corned beef hash
. . . Soups: 2 to 3 cans of family favorites; also, for cooking, cream of mushroom, pea soup, beef consommé, chicken consommé and/or powders for instant broths
. . . Vegetables: 2 to 3 cans of family favorites; mushrooms; French fried onions

CEREALS AND PASTA

. . . Cereal: individual packs
of family favorites
. . . Corn meal (yellow or

white)
. . . Pasta, your favorite
. . . Rice

DAIRY GOODS

. . . Butter (or margarine)
. . . Cheeses: cream cheese;
grated Parmesan or Ro-
mano (or a hunk for you

to grate); your favorite
eating cheeses
. . . Cream (if you use it)
. . . Eggs

FREEZER STOCK (IF YOU HAVE ONE)

. . . Breads: French bread,
rolls, an extra loaf of your
favorite
. . . Extra bacon
. . . Extra butter
. . . Cake or sweet rolls
. . . Ice cream

. . . Meat for 1 to 2 meals
. . . Minced onions
. . . Unbaked pie shell
. . . TV dinners for 1 meal
(the best brand you can
find, which is usually the
costliest)

FRESH PRODUCE

. . . Carrots
. . . Celery
. . . Fruit: anything in season,
allowing at least 1 lb. per
person per weekend
. . . Garlic

. . . Onions
. . . Potatoes, white and/or
sweet
. . . Vegetables: in season, allowing ⅓ to 1 lb. daily
per person

HOUSEHOLD SUPPLIES

. . . Aluminum foil
. . . Baggies
. . . Charcoal (if you barbe-
cue)
. . . Cheesecloth
. . . Cleansing powder
. . . Dust cloths
. . . Facial tissue
. . . Foil broiling pans
. . . Garbage bags
. . . Light bulbs
. . . Matches

. . . Needle & thread
. . . Paper napkins
. . . Paper towels
. . . Saran wrap
. . . Scouring pads
. . . Shampoo
. . . Soap: for dishes, hands,
laundry
. . . Sponges
. . . Toilet paper
. . . Toothpaste
. . . Wax paper

LIQUOR

. . . Your usual assortment, or
. . . ⅕ each of the standards:
    Scotch, bourbon, vodka,
    gin and dry vermouth

. . . Wine: A half gallon each
    of an inexpensive Cali-
    fornia Burgundy and
    Chablis for cooking as
    well as drinking

MEATS

. . . Bacon
. . . Salami
. . . Sausages

. . . Whatever you plan for
    the first few meals

SYRUPS, SWEETS, SNACKS

. . . Gelatins, sweet and plain
. . . Honey
. . . Jams and marmalade
. . . Nuts
. . . Pancake syrup

. . . Peanut butter
. . . Raisins in small treat
    boxes
. . . Sugar, white and brown

SPICES, HERBS, CONDIMENTS

. . . Basil
. . . Bay leaves
. . . Chili powder
. . . Cinnamon
. . . Cloves
. . . Curry powder
. . . Dill
. . . Garlic powder (which I
    prefer to garlic salt)
. . . Ginger

. . . Mustard: dry and
    prepared
. . . Onion powder
. . . Paprika
. . . Parsley flakes
. . . Pepper: cracked black,
    and whole
. . . Salt: regular and coarse
. . . Tarragon, dried

SURVIVAL SHELF (your company emergency shelf)

. . . See description, page 92
. . . See list of foods, Chap-
    ter 5

Index